Ideology & International Relations

George Clarke
(Principal Teacher of Modern Studies, Rockwell High School)

Allan Grieve
(Principal Teacher of Modern Studies, Alloa Academy)

Irene Morrison
(Principal Teacher of Modern Studies, Craigie High School)

Graeme Pont
(Principal Teacher of Modern Studies, Bridge of Don Academy)
(General Editor)

PULSE PUBLICATIONS

CONTENTS

Published and Typeset by
Pulse Publications
45 Raith Road, Fenwick,
Ayrshire, KA3 6DB

Printed by Ritchie of Edinburgh

British Library Cataloguing-in-Publication Data

A Catalogue record for this book is available from
the British Library

ISBN 0 948766 40 9

© Clarke, Grieve, Morrison, & Pont 1996

ACKNOWLEDGEMENTS

The authors and publishers would like to thank the
following for permission to reproduce copyright
material:
Gerry McCann (pages 4, 5, 9, 10, 12, 23, 27);
Telegraph Colour Library (cover and pages 107, 122);
Hulton-Deutsch (pages 43, 59, 85, 94, 101, 103, 105);
PhotoDisk (pages 66, 67, 68, 74, 94, 99)
Charles Smith for material in the USA section.

WHY DO SOME AFRICAN COUNTRIES NEED AID?

What you will learn

1 The differences between developed and developing nations.

2 The needs of some African countries.

3 The reasons why some African countries need aid.

DEVELOPED NATIONS

Industrialised nations such as the United Kingdom, Japan, the USA, France, Germany, the Netherlands and Canada are often referred to as *developed* nations. Typically, such countries share similar social and economic circumstances such as a high standard of living, a good health service, high levels of literacy, low rates of infant mortality and economies based on industry, commerce, insurance and new technology.

Such nations are also referred to as *the rich North.* As a consequence of being rich, with advanced industries, such countries have considerable power. They can affect what happens to the lives of people in many parts of the world—especially in developing continents such as Africa.

DEVELOPING NATIONS

These nations are concentrated in the Southern Hemisphere. Most African countries, India, South American countries and many Asian nations make up this group.

Countries which can be categorised as *developing nations* share similar social and economic problems. Their *needs* are similar. For example, developing nations would share the following: a low standard of living, low levels of health care, high levels of illiteracy, high infant mortality rates and economies which are based on agriculture, a limited range of exports and labour-intensive, poorly skilled means of production. Many of these countries require aid or assistance from developed countries which means that the country giving the aid

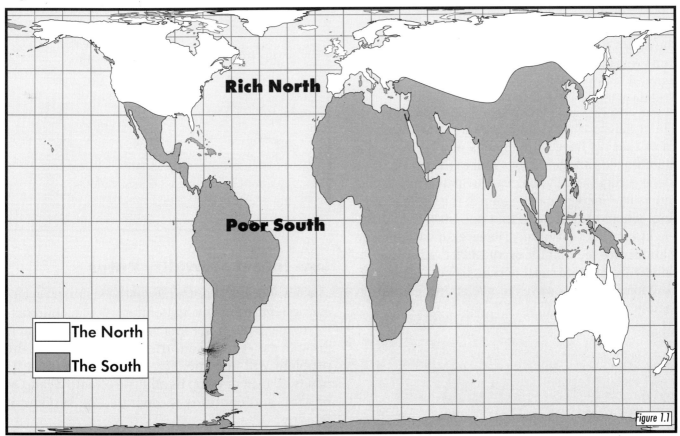

Rich North

Poor South

The North

The South

Figure 1.1

Comparisons between Developed and Developing Nations: Selected Features 1993

	Infant Mortality	Life Expectancy		Population 'Doubling Time'	Per Capita
	(per 1,000 live births)	Males	Females	(in years at current rate)	*GNP 1991 (US$)
DEVELOPED COUNTRIES					
United Kingdom	7.1	73	78	267	16,750
Japan	4.4	76	82	217	26,920
USA	8.6	72	79	92	22,560
France	7.3	73	81	169	20,600
AFRICAN COUNTRIES					
Sudan	87	52	53	22	400
Burkina Faso	119	52	53	21	350
Somalia	127	44	48	22	No data available
Gambia	138	42	46	27	360

*GNP: Gross National Product. This refers to the value of goods produced by a worker in a year, including money gained from trading these goods abroad.

Table 1.1 Source: Population Concern 1993

can have power or influence over the country which receives it.

Such nations are also referred to as *the Third World* or *the Poor South.*

Table 1.1 clearly indicates that the needs of developing and developed nations are different. If we exclude South Africa, the country in sub-Saharan Africa with the highest GNP is Gabon with $3,780, but the infant mortality rate is 112 per 1,000 live births and average life expectancy is 51 for men and 54 for women. Compare these indicators with Japan or France in Table 1.1.

The infant mortality rate is perhaps the best indicator that we have of the needs of a country. If a child's needs are being met well in the first year of life, it is highly likely that there will be a low infant mortality rate. This can be seen in the United Kingdom where only 7.1 children per 1,000 live births die in the first year of life. However, if we consider Gambia, we see that for every 1,000 live births, 138 babies die. This is a startlingly high figure which can be explained by a series of social and economic factors.

Activities

1 What are the main differences between developed and developing nations?

2 What do you think are the three main needs which developing countries share?

3 Which two of the *developed* countries in Table 1.1 are the most successful? Give reasons for your answer.

4 Which two *developing* countries do you feel are most in need of aid? Give reasons for your answer.

5 Explain, using examples, why "Infant mortality rates are perhaps the best indicators of the needs of a country."

Low Infant Mortality Rates

The fewer ticks a country has amongst the seven factors in Figure 1.2, the higher the risk of a child failing to reach his or her first birthday. The less that is done to assist such countries, then the greater the problem will become. For a country to meet its needs, it must develop its ability to create wealth to pay for, and continue to operate, the services it requires.

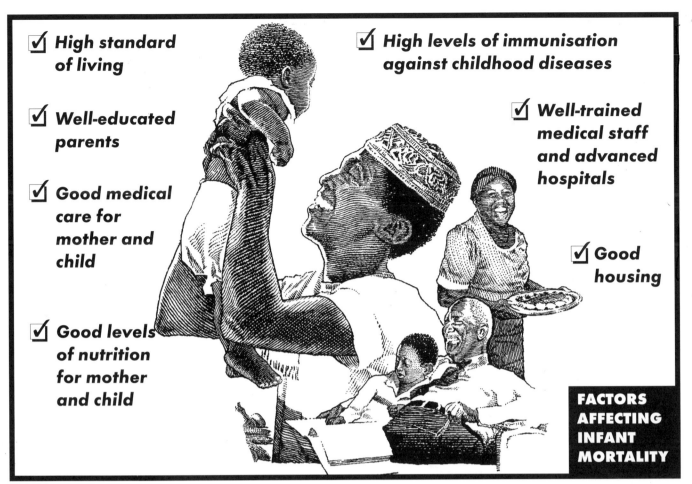

- ☑ **High standard of living**

- ☑ **Well-educated parents**

- ☑ **Good medical care for mother and child**

- ☑ **Good levels of nutrition for mother and child**

- ☑ **High levels of immunisation against childhood diseases**

- ☑ **Well-trained medical staff and advanced hospitals**

- ☑ **Good housing**

FACTORS AFFECTING INFANT MORTALITY

Figure 1.2

Often only a simple action is needed to break into a cycle of poverty or deprivation, leading to a whole series of problems being solved. Figure 1.3 illustrates how one problem can lead to another. However, the cycle can be broken into at a variety of points, thereby changing a cycle of deprivation into a cycle of success.

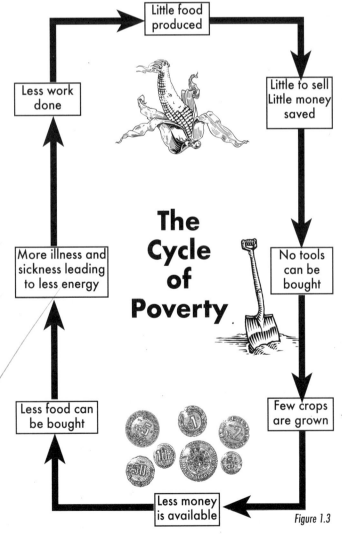

The
**Cycle
of
Poverty**

Little food produced

Little to sell
Little money saved

No tools can be bought

Few crops are grown

Less money is available

Less food can be bought

More illness and sickness leading to less energy

Less work done

Figure 1.3

Activities

1 Explain why any four factors in figure 1.2 could result in lower infant mortality rates.

2 Study the Cycle of Poverty diagram (Figure 1.3). Explain how one problem in the cycle can lead to a series of other problems.

3 Choose one point in the cycle and explain how help or aid at this point could break the cycle.

4 Draw a 'Cycle of Wealth', showing how aid would lead to a change at each stage, resulting in wealth rather than poverty.

3

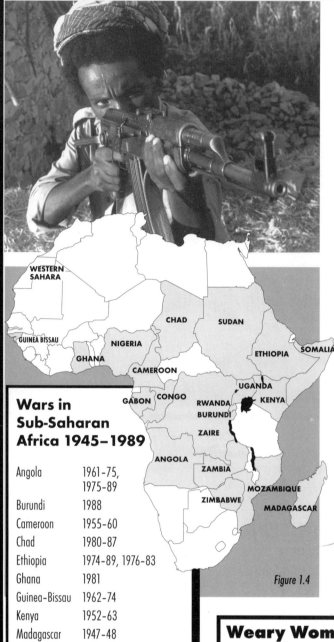

Military Madness

Between 1945 and 1989 sub-Saharan Africa saw at least 30 major military conflicts. Most of the world's military-controlled governments are found in this region.

Military spending

Five of Africa's poorest countries increased their spending on the military between 1972 and 1987 while cutting their spending on social welfare. Table 1.3 below shows the percentage spent on defence and on housing, amenities, social services and welfare.

	Defence		Housing, amenities, social services and welfare	
	1972	1987	1972	1987
Malawi	3.1	6.6	5.8	2.3
Tanzania	11.9	15.8	2.1	1.7
Uganda	23.1	26.3	7.3	2.9
Kenya	6.0	9.1	3.9	1.7
Liberia	5.3	8.9	3.5	1.9

Table 1.3

Figure 1.4

Wars in Sub-Saharan Africa 1945–1989

Angola	1961–75, 1975–89
Burundi	1988
Cameroon	1955–60
Chad	1980–87
Ethiopia	1974–89, 1976–83
Ghana	1981
Guinea-Bissau	1962–74
Kenya	1952–63
Madagascar	1947–48
Mozambique	1965–75, 1981–89
Nigeria	1967–70, 1980–81, 1984
Rwanda	1956–65
Somalia	1988
Sudan	1963–72, 1984–89
Uganda	1966, 1971–78, 1978–79, 1981–87
West Sahara	1975–87
Zaire	1960–65
Zambia	1964
Zimbabwe	1972–79, 1983

Table 1.2

Weary Women

- Women do 75% of Africa's agricultural work and 95% of the domestic work.

- In Mozambique 90% of women are engaged in food production.

- African women do 70% of hoeing and weeding, 60% of harvesting, 50% of planting, 60% of marketing, 90% of food processing and 80% of transporting crops home and storing them.

Unproductive Farming

African agriculture is inefficient. The continent produces an average 2,616 kgs of cereals per acre compared to world levels of 4,800 kgs per acre. Its productivity for roots and tubers is 8,145 kgs per acre compared to 13,236 kgs elsewhere, while it only uses less than 7 kgs of fertiliser per acre of agricultural land compared to over 18 kgs in Latin America and almost 62 kgs in Asia.

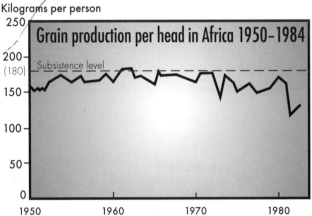

Kilograms per person

Grain production per head in Africa 1950–1984

Subsistence level

Figure 1.6

Plummeting Prices

The prices Africa gets for its primary products slumped sharply in real terms during the 1980s while the prices it had to pay for goods from the west continued to rise.

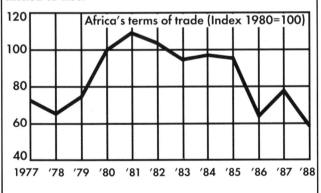

Africa's terms of trade (Index 1980=100)

Figure 1.5

Dominating Debts

Sub-Saharan Africa's total debt increased from about $6 billion in 1970 to $134 billion in 1988. By 1988 the total debt was equal to the region's Gross National Product and was three and a half times its export earnings. Those countries with the largest debts in Black Africa are Nigeria, the Sudan and Ivory Coast.

This table shows the increase in Africa's total debt between 1980 and 1987. Figures are in $US billion.

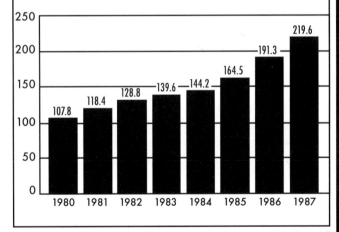

Figure 1.7

Source: *New Internationalist*, June 1990

Activities

Using the information in the Factiles on Africa, write a report on *The Problems Faced in Some African Countries* in which you refer to the following:

    military spending and poverty;   economic problems;   grain production;

    the role of women in African countries.

NB You may wish to use other sources in your school to provide you with further information.

What you will learn

1   The social, economic and political reasons which explain why some African countries experience famine.

2   The reasons why Sudan has experienced food problems.

SOCIAL REASONS

Poverty
Poor Health
Famine
Death
Illiteracy
Low Life
Expectancy

POLITICAL REASONS

ECONOMIC REASONS

Figure 1.8

analysis in mind as we consider why many African countries experience famine.

Social Scientists must look behind the banner head-lines and use the tools of the Sociologist and Political Scientist to offer well-researched explanations which examine the way people live, their economies and their political systems.

Ray Bush, a lecturer in Politics at the University of Leeds, wrote an article entitled *Explaining Africa's Famine.* He challenges the view that it is factors such as climate, drought or crop failure which cause fam-ine (an extreme shortage of food). After all, such cli-matic factors affect other developing countries, but they do not suffer famine to the extent that the Su-dan, Somalia or Ethiopia have over the last ten years.

As a social scientist, Ray Bush looks for *social, eco-nomic* and *political* factors to explain famine. He argues that famine is not caused by 'natural' factors but by 'unnatural' factors created by humankind. In a sentence, he summarises the problem as he sees it: "Famine occurs when the strains on social sys-tems overwhelm the available resources for coping with drought or whatever happens to be the pre-vailing crisis." Simply stated, this means that when a crisis happens, a country cannot respond to solve that crisis because of social, economic and politi-cal factors.

When we see headlines like the ones in Figure 1.9 in our newspapers, it is worth keeping Ray Bush's

RAINS FAIL AGAIN IN ETHIOPIA

MILLIONS FACE DEATH

ANOTHER DROUGHT PREDICTED

$MILLIONS NEEDED

CROPS FAIL IN SUDAN

ANOTHER FAMINE

AFRICA CANNOT COPE WITH ANOTHER DRY SEASON

"As a Social Scientist, I examine Social, Economic and Political factors before arriving at a conclusion. The factfiles on pages 7 and 8 summarise the main concerns I would take account of."

Figure 1.9

FACTFILE 1: Social File

Question: What *Social Factors* would you look at to explain why a country is suffering from food shortages or famine?

Answer: I would consider the following:

- The levels of education in a country. Are literacy rates high or low?

- The customs and habits of a country. Are farming methods adequate? Does the way in which people live lead to certain problems? Are there traditions which prevent development taking place? Are traditional crops the best ones to grow?

- Has there been a drift away from the countryside to the towns, causing unemployment and placing heavy demands on housing, health and other services?

- Are wealth and land concentrated in the hands of a few rich families or merchants?

- Are there major health and medical issues which lead to ill health, early death and an inability to work efficiently?

- What is the attitude towards women? Is the progress of women limited by customs and beliefs?

FACTFILE 2: Economic File

Question: What *Economic Factors* would you look at?

Answer: I would consider the following:

- Is a country in debt to the World Bank or another country? Is that country spending more to repay a loan than it is earning from exports?

- What are the levels of Gross Domestic Product (GDP – the annual value of goods produced and services provided in a country) and Gross National Product (GNP – see page 2) in a particular country?

- How poor are the people? What levels of wages are paid? How high are levels of unemployment?

- What products or raw materials does a country export to generate income? Does it rely on one product or crop where prices can rise and fall leading to financial problems? Is the quality of the product for export of a suitable standard?

- Do multi-national companies control the main industries with profits flowing out of the country back to the developed world? Are the workers of such countries being exploited by the multi-national companies who may be paying very low wages or prices for products?

- Is the aid being given to the country 'Tied Aid'? In other words, does the country receiving aid have to give something back in return?

FACTFILE 3: Political File

Question: What *Political Factors* would you look at?

Answer: I would consider the following:

- Is there war in a country which is causing problems for the economy, eg. land cannot be farmed because of fighting, movement is not possible?

- Is the government in control of the country? Are warring groups stopping aid coming through? Is it safe to transport goods?

- Is a government corrupt? Does it spend aid or money from taxes on the military and police while people starve? Does the government spend money foolishly on great projects like airports which benefit a rich few, while the poor majority starve?

- Does a government persecute groups within its country and abuse their civil rights? For example, are some groups or tribes given better treatment than others?

- Is a government of a communist ideology? If so, does this mean that capitalist nations of the developed world are reluctant to help it?

- Has the government supported enemies of major developed nations like the USA or UK? If so, then this may mean that aid will not be given by developed nations.

Activities

1. Explain why climate, drought or crop failure alone do not cause famine.

2. Use the Social File.

   Explain how any four Social factors could lead to food shortages.

3. Use the Economic File.

   (a) Explain how any four Economic factors could lead to food shortages.

   (b) Which of the Economic factors you mentioned is the most important? Give reasons for your answer.

4. Use the Political File.

   (a) Explain how any four Political factors could lead to food shortages.

   (b) Do you agree that Economic factors are the main causes of food shortages? Using the FACTFILES, give detailed reasons to support your view.

CASE STUDY – Sudan

FACTFILE: The Sudan

Demography

Population:	25,195,000 (1990)
Urban:	22%
Density:	10 inhabitants/sq km.
Annual growth:	2.9% (1990–99)
Estimate for year 2000:	33 million
Children per woman:	6.4

SUDAN

Health Services

One physician for every 5,740 inhabitants (1986) and one hospital bed for every 1,120 (1986).

Under-five mortality: 175 per 1,000 (1989).

Calorie consumption: 88% of required intake (1984–86).

Safe water: 21% of the population has access (1985–88).

Education

Literacy (1990):
Male: 43%
Female: 12%

School Enrolment: (1986)
Primary: 49%
Secondary: 20%
University: 246 students per 100,000 inhabitants

Primary school teachers: one for every 35 students (1986)

Economy

Per capita GNP:	$480 (1988)
Annual growth:	4.2% (1980–88)
Annual inflation:	33.5% (1980–87)
Cereal imports:	702,000 metric tons (1987–88)
Food import dependency:	15%
Imports:	$1.2 billion (1990)
Exports:	$672 million (1989)
Major export products:	cotton 34%; crude vegetable materials 17%; live animals 12%; cereals 10%; oil seeds 8%.
Major markets:	EU 29%; South & South East Asia 21%; West Asia 15%; Eastern Europe & ex-USSR 9%.
External debt:	$13.0 billion; $515 per capita (1989).
Development aid received:	$760 million (1989); $31 per capita.

Armed Forces

56,750 members (1989)

Paramilitary: 3,000

Source: Various

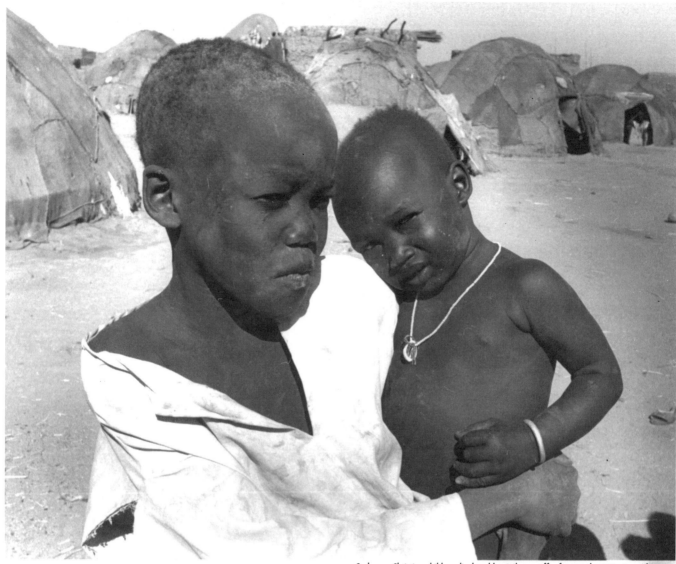

Sudanese Christian children displaced by civil war suffer from malnutrition in a Khartoum shanty town.

WHY HAS SUDAN SUFFERED FAMINE?

Famine does not occur simply because of problems with the climate. Sudan is a classic example of how Social, Economic and Political factors have combined to leave the majority of the population in Sudan poor and on the threshold of starvation.

Throughout the 1970s, 1980s and into the 1990s, Sudan faced a succession of problems which we will examine in this case study. Sudan faced famine in 1983, 1984, 1985 and 1992. In 1996, the problems still continued.

Social Factors

Despite the fact that Sudan is the size of Europe and the largest country in Africa, much of the land is marginal which means that only some land is of a quality to grow crops. The good land is owned by only a few rich merchants which leads to extremes of wealth and poverty. Only a few big merchants control the grain in Sudan and they fix the prices and direct distribution.

There were changes in long-established habits which led to the traditional efficient earth mound grain stores being replaced by large-scale collection by the government. When famine arrived, the grain stores were found to be empty as the government had sold the grain for profit, leaving the Sudanese people without food.

In the countryside, there was massive overfarming which led to the land becoming exhausted. In addition, more modern mechanised methods of farming led to large-scale rural unemployment. The new methods did not take care of the land, so leaving Sudan more vulnerable to famine. The thousands of people who were now without work were forced to look elsewhere for employment.

As a consequence of the changes in farming methods, there has been a large-scale drift to the towns in order to look for work. However, there is little chance of finding work and over 25% of the children there suffer from malnutrition.

Sudan has now become aid dependent, with 90% of its cattle dead as a result of drought. Cattle constituted the traditional means of *trade* and *exchange* in rural areas. As a result, with 90% of the cattle gone, the people in these areas do not have the means to buy food.

Economic Factors

We could examine numerous economic factors, but the examination of one example highlights some major issues.

The Gazira is a very fertile area of land in Sudan with enormous agricultural potential.

In the 1970s Sudan grew more food than it needed and was more than self-sufficient. In fact, there was a *surplus* of food which was stored or exported.

The IMF and World Bank were approached by Sudan for a major loan. A condition of granting this loan was that cotton production, rather than food production, should be developed. This would ensure that the loan, with interest, would be repaid. (Also, a market was created for USA grain of which there was a surplus.)

However, in the '70s and '80s the cotton market collapsed, leaving Sudan with cotton it could not sell. Sudan was now committed to buying imported wheat from the USA (which wanted to expand its wheat market to satisfy the demands of US farm-

ers) despite the fact that it is cheaper for Sudan to grow wheat, rather than to import it.

Political Factors

Of all factors working against the relief of famine in Sudan, political factors are perhaps the most important. The situation is complex but the following facts will help to create a full picture.

In 1989, Lieutenant-General Omar Hassan al-Bashir came to power by overthrowing the civilian government. Islamic Fundamentalism guides his government's actions with Islamic law controlling people's lives. Strict laws, such as cutting off the hands of thieves are in force.

A civil war with the Christian majority in the South continues, with allegations that Hassan al-Bashir's government is strangling supplies of food aid to the rebels in the South. Many feel he wishes to crush those of the Christian faith.

As a result of civil war, an estimated three to four million refugees have moved North towards the capital, Khartoum, causing even greater problems of overcrowding, unemployment and starvation.

In 1989, Oxfam and Save the Children Fund stated that the Darfur region of Sudan was heading for the biggest famine in Africa's history *but* urgently needed Food Aid from Western governments was not forthcoming. The West opposed the military government in Sudan which had overthrown the democratically elected government. Furthermore, Sudan had backed Saddam Hussein against the West during the Gulf War in 1991. The USA, for a time, had cut off all relations with Sudan in response to its support of Iraq.

Western countries would only give aid if the government of Sudan came out into the open and admitted there was a famine in the Darfur Region. Sudan would not do this, so aid was not given. The government could not admit the truth, and the government-controlled news media claimed bumper harvests in Sudan and no famine in Darfur!

This meant that emergency aid from the West was suspended, resulting in starvation and an escalation of the problems in Sudan.

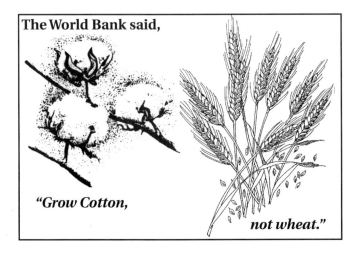

The World Bank said,

"Grow Cotton,

not wheat."

Sudan Zealots Wreak Terror on Aid Teams

by Christina Lamb

INTERNATIONAL relief agencies are accusing the Sudanese authorities of carrying out a terror campaign to force them out of the country.

They believe that the Islamic dictatorship wants to rid Sudan of Western aid organisations as part of its Islamic programme. They say it wants all relief work to be carried out by Islamic agencies which use food aid as a bribe to win converts and allegedly use some of the donations to pay for the war against rebels in Sudan's mostly Christian South.

Ghazi Salehuddin, political adviser to President Omar Hassan al-Bashir, admitted the government would prefer aid to be carried out by Islamic organisations.

Salehuddin insists Sudan needs no outside help. "Our motto is independence and that means being independent of foreign aid, foreign policies and foreign will."

Adapted from *The Sunday Times*, 28.8.94

Activities

1 Study the Sudan Factfile on page 9. What conclusions do you come to about Sudan?

2 What role have the following Social factors had in creating famine in Sudan:

land ownership;

farming methods;

drift to the towns?

3 What part did the IMF and the World Bank play in creating food shortages in Sudan?

4 Why can it be said that Political factors are the most important causes of famine in Sudan?

5 Why do some international relief agencies believe that the views of the government leaders in Sudan are a major cause of problems?

PHOTOFILE: Children at Work & Play

WHY IS AID GIVEN BY DEVELOPED NATIONS?

What you will learn

1 The main sources of aid for African countries.

2 The types of aid given to African countries.

3 The social, economic and political reasons which explain why developed countries give aid.

4 The ways in which the British government helps to meet the needs of some African countries.

WHAT IS AID?

Aid is help which can assist a country to overcome problems it faces. It can be long-term, short-term or medium-term. The types of aid are numerous and *good aid* focuses on the problems of a particular country and targets aid to solve problems by listening to the people who are suffering and responding to them. Increasingly, the slogan 'Trade not Aid' has been adopted as the best way of helping developing countries. (See Section 5, page 25)

Aid comes from three main sources:

1 From the governments of developed nations.

2 From international organisations such as the United Nations (see Section 4).

3 From voluntary organisations such as Oxfam, Christian Aid, Save the Children Fund etc.

Activities

1 Draw up and complete a table like the one below. Discuss this first with a partner, or as part of a group.

Type of Aid	Advantages	Disadvantages
Financial Aid		
Specialist Workers, Experts		
Equipment		
Emergency Relief Aid		
Food Aid		
Military Aid		

2 Which two types of aid do you feel are the best long-term solutions? Give reasons for your answers.

3 Which two types of aid do you feel are the best short-term solutions? Give reasons for your answers.

TYPES OF AID

Financial Aid

This can involve loans of money which have to be paid back with interest; grants which do not have to be paid back; subsidies to assist exports; trade deals.

Specialist Workers and Experts

Teachers, trainers, medical professionals and specialist advisers can be sent. Researchers and managers are also useful as they can organise and plan training programmes.

Equipment

Specialist equipment to aid development can be sent, such as: vehicles, farming equipment, engineering parts, manufacturing equipment.

Food Aid

Surplus products such as cereals, powdered milk, grain and dairy products can be sent. Often, food aid is part of emergency relief aid projects.

Military Aid

To support a friendly government facing attack or the threat of attack, such things as guns, tanks, various other weapons, military advisers and peace keeping forces can be sent.

Emergency Relief Aid

The Tribune — FAMINE IN HORN OF AFRICA — Ethiopia — Somalia

This aid is sent to assist with disasters such as earthquakes, floods and droughts. By sending immediate assistance such as tents, medical supplies, food and clothing, short-term help is given to deal with immediate problems.

All aid is either *bilateral aid* or *multilateral aid*. Bilateral aid is aid given by one country to another country. An example is shown in figure 1.10.

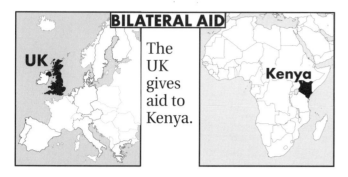

Figure 1.10

Multilateral aid is aid given by a *group* of countries, eg. aid given by the United Nations (UN) or the European Union (EU) (see Figure 1.11). In 1984 the EU agreed the Dublin Plan. This gave aid to 8 badly affected countries. By 1986, one-third of all aid given to sub-Saharan Africa came from EU members.

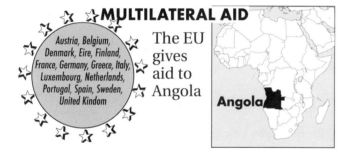

Figure 1.11

TIED AID

When *bilateral* aid is given, there are usually conditions attached to the giving of that aid. For example, a country in Africa may be given a grant from Britain, but in return a proportion of that money has to be spent on British goods and services. Such aid, therefore, has 'strings attached'. Hence it is re-

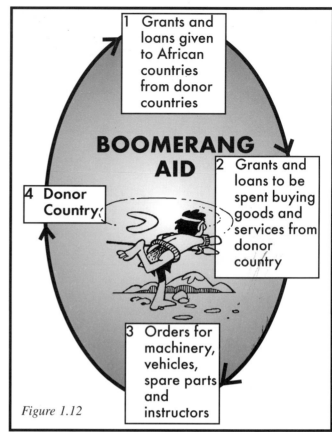

Figure 1.12

ferred to as *tied aid*. (NB. A grant of money does not have to be paid back; a loan has to be paid back with interest.)

Sometimes tied aid is referred to as *boomerang aid* because, like a boomerang, it returns to the person who sent it. (see figure 1.12)

Focus on Tied Aid

Many observers have noted that there are serious problems associated with tied aid. These people may make the following statements:

" It might help the donor country more than the country receiving it."

" It may be aid which is not appropriate to the needs of the African country receiving the aid."

" The country receiving aid can be forced into buying goods and services which are more expensive than those to be found in a competitive marketplace."

" It has been calculated that the real value of aid to a country is reduced by up to one-third if conditions are attached to the giving of that aid."

" The donor country can become involved in a power relationship with the country receiving the aid, with the donor being in a position to control events in the recipient country."

Activities

1 What is the difference between Bilateral and Multilateral aid?

2 Say if each of the following is an example of Bilateral or Multilateral aid:

(a) The USA sends tractors to Ethiopia.

(b) France sends doctors to Senegal.

(c) The EU agrees to send surplus grain to Mozambique.

(d) The UN sends medical supplies to Rwanda.

(e) A group of Scandinavian countries agrees to send farming experts to Gabon.

3 What points is the cartoon on page 14 making about some types of aid?

4 What is tied aid?

5 What criticisms can be made of tied aid?

6 Provide arguments in favour of tied aid.

7 Overall, what is your view of tied aid?

WHY DO DEVELOPED COUNTRIES GIVE AID TO AFRICAN COUNTRIES?

There are a variety of Social, Economic and Political reasons for giving aid. There are also *humanitarian* reasons whereby a country is so moved by the suffering and horror in another country that for reasons of compassion or pity, aid is sent. Humanitarian reasons can also be grouped under *social* reasons. Such aid is often in response to public pressure after horrific accounts of starvation and suffering reported by the news media, eg. Michael Buerk's BBC TV report on Ethiopia in the 1980s and reports from Rwanda in 1995.

Social Factors

We would take into account a number of issues before giving aid. For example, we would look at levels of literacy in a country: how low are they? We would also examine a range of factors such as birth rates, death rates and levels of health care. If these were very poor we would consider what help could be given. We must consider if the needs of one country are greater than those of another.

We might examine the way the land is managed and the farming methods used. We have expertise which we could give to help overcome poor farming practices. We would, of course, take account of *humanitarian* factors and seek to relieve extreme suffering caused by a crop failure or climatic changes.

Economic Factors

We must consider financial matters. If our economy is poor and trade is bad, then we will not have enough money from our taxes to give as much as we wish. On the other hand, we might be able to reduce the level of our unemployment by developing trade based on tied aid.

If a developing country is poor, but rich in natural resources, we may give aid and in return we could make use of these natural resources. If giving aid to a country could help to develop trade links which could benefit us, then we would consider giving assistance.

We must be sensible and consider whether or not a country would pay back any loan we might give. Nevertheless, at the end of the day we must look at our own economy and if we have high rates of inflation with accompanying demands on our social services, we may not have as much money to give in aid as we might wish. We must consider the needs of our own people at home.

Political Factors

Political factors are important when we consider whether to give aid to a country or not. If a country is undemocratic or has a bad record on human rights, we would be reluctant to help that country. The ideology of the government is important too, for if it were a communist government, we in the West would not wish to support such a regime because communism works against our capitalist beliefs. It would be foolish to support an ideology we did not approve of.

If a country is at war we would have to decide which side, if any, we would support. Also, if it were too dangerous we would not send over aid workers. An important factor would be the views of our allies. We would not be keen to give aid to a country which was hostile to one of our friendly allies. This could offend our allies and cause problems for us.

On the home front, we would have to consider the views of our people. If giving support to a country was unpopular with voters, then they may vote against us in a general election. We certainly would not want that!

Giving aid is not as simple as some people believe.

Activities

Imagine you are a senior politician being interviewed by a television journalist.

Script an interview in which you respond to questions asking you about the factors you take into account before deciding whether or not to give aid.

Emphasise those factors which seem to you to be the most important.

CASE STUDY: Britain's overseas aid and 'good government'

In 1991 the British Government stated that its policy on giving aid would require that a country was progressing towards 'good government'. What is 'good government'?

Baroness Lynda Chalker, the Minister for Overseas Development, defined good government as having the following features:

- It does not undertake excessive spending on the military.

- It provides competent administration.

- It should be democratic.

- It must respect human rights and the rule of law.

- It allows an economic free market where the government does not control and own industry.

What does this policy mean in practice?

■ If a country does not demonstrate the features of good government and if it is not working towards good government, humanitarian aid would still be given but not development aid.

■ In 1991, £28 million was spent on direct help for good government. In 1991-92 a target of £50 million was set, eg. £5 million of the aid given to Zambia was given to develop local government.

■ Kenya's president, Daniel Arap Moi, announced his opposition to what he saw as interference by Britain in the internal affairs of other countries.

■ Some see the policy as a threat by Britain, giving it power to control governments in foreign countries.

■ Some say it is an attempt by Britain to cut its overseas aid budget.

■ Others believe that it is almost impossible for a country to meet all the conditions laid down by Britain to meet the 'good government' standards.

This approach to aid, as you can see, has provoked considerable criticism. However, it is important for you to consider the issues and arrive at your own conclusion.

British aid at work

60% of British aid is bilateral and 76% of aid goes to the poorest countries. Of the top twenty recipients of bilateral aid in 1990, eleven were African. (see table 1.4)

African countries receiving British aid in 1990

COUNTRY	£ million
Kenya	44.4
Malawi	37.2
Mozambique	25.4
Zambia	24.5
Uganda	24.0
Tanzania	23.2
Sudan	21.4
Zimbabwe	20.7
Ethiopia	20.0
Ghana	19.9
Guyana	15.3

Table 1.4   Source: ODA

CASE STUDY: British aid to Mozambique

Figure 1.13

Mozambique is one of the poorest countries in Africa. A prolonged war added to an already serious situation. Britain has identified Mozambique as a country in need of aid.

Britain's aid is attempting to promote economic recovery in a number of ways. For example, spare parts, raw materials and improvements in the transport system all feature in Britain's aid package. Although emergency relief has been given, the emphasis of the aid is long-term, designed to help build up the economy of Mozambique.

British aid has been in the form of grants rather than loans, so Mozambique does not have to pay back the money given plus interest.

Since 1983, British bilateral aid to Mozambique has been in the form of grants. It has included:

➡ £14 million provided to improve the railway network (1989);

➡ Port improvement projects to assist exports;

➡ Bridge building and road building programmes;

➡ Education schemes including developing courses and teacher training;

➡ Programme aid such as: medical supplies, trucks, parts for power generators, pesticides for cotton, assistance to industry.

The Overseas Development Administration (ODA) is the body through which British government aid is channelled. The aims of the ODA are discussed in the extract *A Partnership in Development.* on page 18. Bearing these aims in mind, more detailed examples of British aid to Mozambique are outlined below.

Maputo port is an important outlet for goods to many areas. Britain has helped to restore the war-ravaged port in the following ways:

➡ provided experts in areas of transportation and container handling;

➡ helped to improve the way that finance is dealt with;

➡ trained port staff;

➡ provided new cargo handling and workshop equipment;

➡ rebuilt areas of the port.

Energy

✳ supplied spare parts and replacements for British generators which produce electricity for areas in Mozambique;

✳ provided consultants and experts;

✳ donated £4.8 million to upgrade steam turbines to improve the supply of electricity.

Programme Aid

This is aid which is planned specifically to develop the economy of Mozambique. The programme is called the Economic Rehabilitation Programme and includes the following:

✚ since 1985, more than £40 million has been sent to pay for imports of equipment, spare parts and raw materials;

✚ drugs, medical supplies, and pesticides have been provided;

✚ trucks, spare parts for tractors, parts for power generators have been supplied;

✚ equipment and raw materials to produce goods such as batteries, pens, biscuits and other products for sale have been sent.

In addition to these specific examples, ODA assistance has concentrated on Transport, Fisheries, Education and Training and cooperation with the World Bank, the European Union and the African Development Bank. The African Development Bank provides aid to the sugar industry and for the development of banking practices in Mozambique.

In short, the ODA seeks to be involved in long-term aid projects and applies the 'Good Government' principle when selecting which countries shall receive development aid.

The fall and fall of British aid

A LANDMARK for British relationships with the Third World in 1990 was the record inflow of £6,847 million ($10,612 million) from repayments on previous debts by developing countries.

It meant a net inflow of funds from the poor world, after overseas aid and investments had been deducted, of £2,600 million ($4,030 million). This was the first time for the UK that repayments on past loans exceeded official aid and new loans.

As a percentage of gross national product, Britain has halved its aid to developing countries in the last 30 years. In 1960 the British government gave 0.56 per cent of GNP in development aid; in 1990 it gave 0.27 per cent. In both years a Conservative government was in power. Between 1960 and 1990 the standard of living measured in terms of GNP per head roughly doubled.

Since Conservative government resumed in 1979, British aid has fallen sharply–by a third. However it also fell under the Labour administration of 1964–

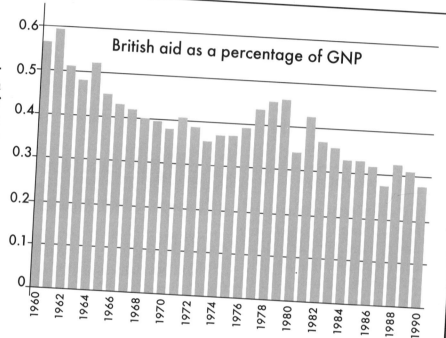

British aid as a percentage of GNP

1970 from 0.53 per cent to 0.37 per cent. Nevertheless, the Socialists deserve half a bouquet. For when Labour was in office from 1974 to 1979, at a time of great economic crisis, aid rose from 0.37 per cent to 0.45 per cent.

As for the future, British government aid plans announced in November 1992 project a slight increase from £1,835 million ($2,845 million) for 1992/93 to £1,900 million ($3,515 million) for 1993/94. It will then be frozen for the next two years. In case anyone needs reminding, the pledge given by all donor countries, including Britain, at the Rio Summit in June 1992 was to reach the UN aid target of 0.7 per cent of GNP "as soon as possible".

Source: *International Agricultural Development*, Vol 12, No 6 1992

CHAPTER 1

HOW THE UN HELPS TO MEET THE NEEDS OF AFRICAN COUNTRIES

What you will learn

1 The reasons for the United Nations giving aid to African countries.

2 How UN specialised agencies can help African countries to meet their needs.

3 How UNICEF can help to meet the needs of some African children.

4 How particular African countries have benefited from United Nations aid.

In June 1945, the aims of the United Nations (UN) were established. Fifty countries signed the charter which set out what the aims of the UN were. Each country promised to abide by the aims when it signed the UN Charter.

The horrors of the Second World War had made many world leaders determined to create a more peaceful, safe and fair world. President Roosevelt of the USA came up with the name United Nations in 1942, but it was not until 1945 that the UN was established.

The key idea guiding the formation of the UN was to provide a forum whereby nations of the world could work together and cooperate to improve the conditions of people in the world.

Aims of the United Nations

1 To maintain international peace and security, while trying to achieve cooperation amongst the nations of the world.

2 To achieve, through cooperation, the protection of human rights in all countries of the world.

3 To cooperate in order to promote economic and social progress throughout the world.

4 To be a focus in the world in order to promote the above aims and to be a centre for organising the methods by which the UN's aims can be realised.

From its small beginning in 1945 with fifty mem-

THE UNITED NATIONS

The work of the UN can be reduced to three vital areas, with each contributing to some particular aspect of the UN's aims.

Working for human rights and freedoms.

Keeping and developing world peace.

Encouraging social and economic progress.

Summary of the Universal Declaration of Human Rights

1 All human beings are born free and equal.

2 Everyone has the right to life, liberty and security.

3 No one shall be held as a slave.

4 No one shall be subjected to torture or to cruel, inhuman or degrading treatment or punishment.

5 No one shall suffer arrest without legal cause.

6 Everyone has the right to own property, live in peace, have a decent standard of living and also the right to work and education.

Figure 1.15

bers, the UN had grown to 184 members by 1995. Underpinning the work of the UN is a fundamental belief in Human Rights, as set out in the 1940 Universal Declaration of Human Rights (see Figure 1.14).

In this section of the book, our main focus is on how the UN works towards, and encourages, social and economic progress. This is achieved through the work of a variety of Specialised Agencies.

Activities

1 In what ways might the aims of the United Nations be of help to developing African countries?

2 Read Aim 6 of the Universal Declaration of Human Rights. In what ways might the United Nations work to achieve this aim?

UNITED NATIONS SPECIALISED AGENCIES

In order to meet its aims and principles, the United Nations works through a series of Specialised Agencies. Each has special skills and expertise to help meet the needs of developing nations. The Specialised Agencies which can be of most help to developing countries are shown in Figure XX.

Food and Agricultural Organisation

UNITED NATIONS SPECIALISED AGENCIES

International Labour Organisation

UNESCO

United Nations Educational, Scientific and Cultural Organisation

United Nations Children's Fund

World Health Organisation

Figure 1.15

Factfile: WHO

The WHO is there to meet medical needs by promoting good health and good medical facilities.

The WHO has been involved in numerous projects in Africa which have included the following:

- Helping governments to set up health services.
- Training health professionals such as doctors, nurses, midwives and health visitors.
- Developing primary health care at local village level where hospitals and doctors are not readily available.
- Researching and working on health problems, eg. AIDS.
- Mass immunisation campaigns.

Factfile: FAO

The FAO specialises in trying to raise levels of nutrition and in working on methods of improving the food supply by farmers. African projects have included the following:

- Helping governments to train people to work on programmes aimed at improving crop yields, nutrition and the quality of crops.
- Researching and developing farming methods which can be applied to local conditions. Such projects have involved new irrigation schemes, using high yield crops, applying appropriate fertilisers and developing fisheries, forestry and cattle farming.
- Introducing new knowledge, equipment and modern methods of farming.
- Supplying experts, advisers and educators.

Factfile: UNESCO

UNESCO is concerned with developing education in its broadest possible sense. As well as attempting to improve literacy levels, other areas such as science and the arts are promoted. Projects in Africa have included:

- Encouraging governments to establish education systems which are compulsory for all.
- Sending advisers and teachers/lecturers to help create high quality schooling.
- Carrying out research in areas such as education, science and communication.
- Working to save works of art, monuments, areas of historic interest and the dying culture and social systems of tribal groups.
- Encouraging cooperation in arts and culture between African countries and the rest of the world.

Factfile: ILO

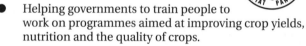

The ILO is concerned with trying to improve working conditions. Frequently in African countries wages are low, safety conditions are poor and workers, often children, are exploited. The ILO has been involved in addressing the following:

- Improving conditions of work and attempting to improve health and safety.
- Helping young children who may be forced to work for over 12 hours a day.
- Researching conditions and offering models of good practice to those who run factories and businesses.

UNICEF's function is to help children in need, and also to help the mothers of these children. It focuses on a variety of different areas which include the following:

- Organising emergency relief for children after a disaster.
- Working with WHO to set up medical facilities and programmes such as immunisation, birth control advice or establishing health centres.
- Projects to help mother and child such as their breast feeding campaign, education campaigns and safe motherhood campaigns.
- School projects to lower the high rates of illiteracy in many African countries.

Activities

1 Which UN Specialised Agency could help to deal with each of the following problems?

(a) Overfarmed land.

(b) Outdated, traditional farming methods.

(c) High rates of illiteracy.

(d) An outbreak of polio.

(e) Dangerous machinery in a fruit packing factory.

(f) Starving children.

2 Which two Specialised Agencies do you feel could be of most help to developing countries in Africa? Give detailed reasons for your choices.

3 Write a report on the United Nations Specialised Agencies. Use the following headings:

The main UN Specialised Agencies;

Ways in which the UN can help to reduce famine;

Examples of good aid;

Ways in which people are helped to help themselves.

UNICEF IN ACTION IN AFRICA

Sub-Saharan Africa

1000 Km
1000 Miles

Figure 1.16

The problems of Sub-Saharan Africa are summarised below.

- Women have an average of 6.5 children.
- Mothers have a 1 in 20 chance of dying in childbirth.
- 183 children die for every 1,000 live births.
- 31% of children suffer from poor nourishment.
- 48% of children reach Primary 5 level of schooling.
- The population could triple from 550 million by the year 2025.
- The population growth of 3% per year outstrips the region's agricultural and economic growth.

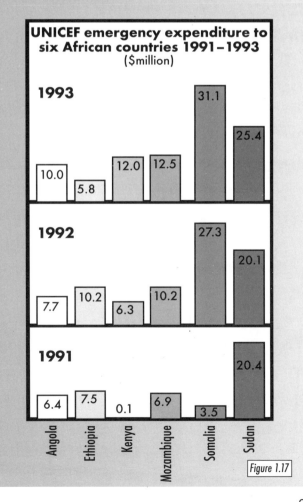

UNICEF emergency expenditure to six African countries 1991–1993
($million)

1993

Angola	Ethiopia	Kenya	Mozambique	Somalia	Sudan
10.0	5.8	12.0	12.5	31.1	25.4

1992

Angola	Ethiopia	Kenya	Mozambique	Somalia	Sudan
7.7	10.2	6.3	10.2	27.3	20.1

1991

Angola	Ethiopia	Kenya	Mozambique	Somalia	Sudan
6.4	7.5	0.1	6.9	3.5	20.4

Figure 1.17

At a meeting of the Organisation of African Unity (OAU) in November 1992, a series of targets to help children were set. UNICEF backed these goals, which included the following:

- Expanding immunisation programmes.

- Oral Rehydration Therapy (ORT) to help children with diarrhoea. A solution of water, salt and sugar can replace the fluids lost, so saving lives.

- Salt iodisation (providing iodine) to avoid mental and physical handicap.

In 1993, in Angola, Somalia, Mozambique and Rwanda, war or conflict caused serious problems for children. In Angola it is estimated that 1.5 million children were affected. Extreme problems can be experienced in getting emergency aid through when there are battles, bombings, land mines and shootings. However, UNICEF had some success in each of these countries.

In Angola UNICEF achieved the folowing:

- 860,000 children and women were vaccinated.

- Vitamin A supplements were given to more than 400,000 children.

- 1 million families received seeds and tools.

- In the town of Malange, feeding programmes and shelter were provided for 30,000 abandoned children.

UNICEF achieved the following in Somalia:

- More than 500 community health workers were trained.

- 158 traditional birth workers were trained.

- Immunisation centres were set up throughout the country.

- 750,000 children received the measles vaccination.

- Water systems, wells and ventilated pit latrines were constructed.

UNICEF achieved the following in Mozambique:

- Helped to resettle millions of refugees and displaced people who had lost their homes as a result of war in that country.

- 750,000 tools and 3,500 metric tons of seeds were distributed to 200,000 people.

- Water was brought to drought-affected areas.

- Over 135,000 women and children were immunised.

FACTFILE: African Children

CHILDBIRTH

In Africa, 1 in 20 women die in childbirth, a large number when you consider that 500,000 women around the world die as a consequence of giving birth. In developed countries only 1 in 3,600 women die in childbirth.

In addition to the many deaths, millions of women suffer disabling injuries caused by childbirth. A lack of vitamin A accounts for 20–30% of young child deaths.

Many girls face prejudice in developing countries and receive less food, medical care and education than boys. This adds to the problems faced by both women and their children during and after childbirth.

BIRTH RATE (per 1,000 of Population)	
Sudan	45
Ethiopia	47
Malawi	53
Mozambique	45
United Kingdom	14

INFANT MORTALITY RATE (per 1,000 live births)	
Sudan	87.0
Ethiopia	127.0
Malawi	138.0
Mozambique	151.0
United Kingdom	7.1

LIFE EXPECTANCY AT BIRTH	Male	Female
Sudan	52	53
Ethiopia	44	48
Malawi	46	49
Mozambique	45	48
United Kingdom	73	78

POPULATION UNDER AGE 15 (%)	
Sudan	46
Ethiopia	49
Malawi	48
Mozambique	44
United Kingdom	19

MARRIED WOMEN USING CONTRACEPTION (%)	
Sudan	9
Ethiopia	4
Malawi	7
Mozambique	–
United Kingdom	81

GROSS NATIONAL PRODUCT (GNP) (per capita USA$)	
Sudan	400
Ethiopia	120
Malawi	230
Mozambique	70
United Kingdom	16,750

Table 1.5   Source: Population Concern, 1993

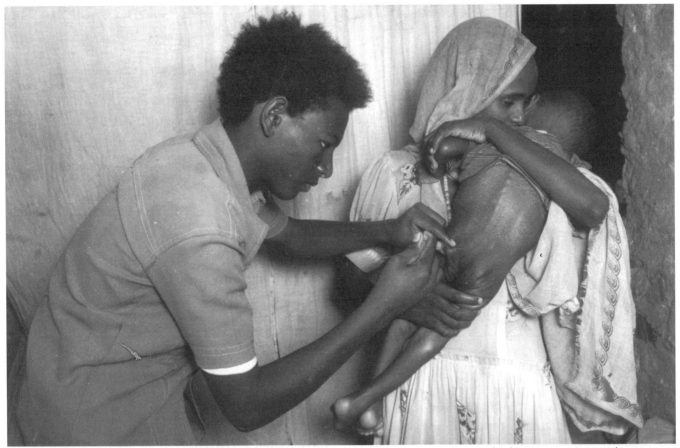

Aid worker in Vaccination Centre in Ethiopian war zone

THE BAMAKO INITIATIVE

The Bamako Initiative is an organised effort to expand Primary Health Care (PHC). PHC is the medical care given by health workers to prevent illness or disease and the education they give to help people to remain healthy.

The initiative supports governments and encourages them to develop their PHC and strengthen it where such provision already exists. It also tries to develop links between hospitals dealing with child-related medical conditions. Links have been established between PHC services and schools, religious groups, women's groups and youth groups.

Around 30 countries are involved in the Bamako Initiative, with four more African countries joining in 1994: Burkina Faso, Chad, Niger and Sudan.

Below are two case studies where the Bamako Initiative has brought great benefits for a low cost.

CASE STUDY 1 — BENIN

The Bamako Initiative has meant that the health service has been improved greatly, with all health policy relying on the Bamako Initiative for its present and future success.

With UNICEF support, 200 health centres, covering around 58% of the total population, have changed their health policies. For example, community cost-sharing has been adopted with costs being spread amongst various communities. The ability to keep funding such health centres is important for the future and with UNICEF's help, 85% of health centres have been able to recover all costs, including the drugs bill.

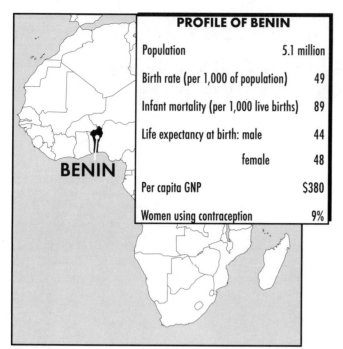

Figure 1.18

PROFILE OF BENIN	
Population	5.1 million
Birth rate (per 1,000 of population)	49
Infant mortality (per 1,000 live births)	89
Life expectancy at birth: male	44
female	48
Per capita GNP	$380
Women using contraception	9%

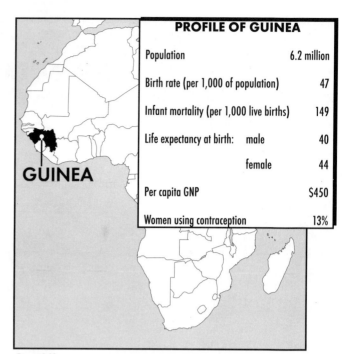

Figure 1.19

PROFILE OF GUINEA	
Population	6.2 million
Birth rate (per 1,000 of population)	47
Infant mortality (per 1,000 live births)	149
Life expectancy at birth: male	40
female	44
Per capita GNP	$450
Women using contraception	13%

By June 1993, 86% of people had received BCG immunisation, 71% had been immunised against Polio, with equally large numbers being given the DPT (Diptheria, Polio and Tetanus) innoculation. A great success, with implications for the long-term future, was the fact that 75% of pregnant women obtained medical consultations before the birth of their children. In addition, 63% of births were attended by skilled medical staff.

Probably the greatest success of all is the fact that, in a country where per capita GNP is only $380, the cost per patient for a visit to a health centre was only $0.50.

UNICEF identified the medical needs of the people of Benin and, by working with the people, provided appropriate aid. This is a good example of UNICEF working with the people of a country and listening to their priorities.

CASE STUDY 2 – GUINEA

Guinea is another example of an African country where the whole nation has had its health service improved by working with UNICEF. The Bamako Initiative has, again, been very successful.

Progress has been remarkable and has been achieved over a surprisingly short period of time. For example, in 1987 there were only 31 health centres in the country and less than 5% of the children of Guinea had been immunised. As a result of participating in the Bamako Initiative, six years later in

1993 there had been a substantial improvement with a total of 265 health centres being established. It was expected that, by 1995, the number would have increased to 340.

In the area of immunisation, results have been equally spectacular with 76% coverage for BCG, 70% protection against tetanus for pregnant women and 57% protection of children against measles. Other illnesses had immunisation rates of between 55 and 72%. This will have a major impact on the extremely high infant mortality rate and overall life expectancy which, at 40 for males, is one of the lowest in Africa.

Activities

1   Imagine you are a newspaper reporter, writing a series of articles on the Bamako Initiative. Your editor has given you the following outline which you must use when writing your reports:

What is the Bamako Initiative?

What is happening in Benin; what were its problems and what has been done?

How do Guinea's problems compare with those in Benin?

What has the UN done to help in Guinea?

2   Overall, what is your view of the Bamako Initiative?

CHAPTER 1

What you will learn

1 The differences between good and bad aid.

2 The extent to which aid can help developing countries.

APPROPRIATE AID AND INAPPROPRIATE AID

Does aid work? The short answer is 'not always'. We can distinguish between aid which is useful and aid which is not useful to the receiving country.

Good Aid

Aid given by richer countries is said to be helpful when it satisfies some of the following points.

✔ The people receiving the aid are consulted.

✔ The aid helps people to become self-sufficient and so frees them from the need to ask for aid in the future.

✔ The aid is targeted to meet specific needs and is designed to help people.

✔ The aid is monitored and assessed to examine how effective it is.

Bad Aid

Aid given by richer countries is unhelpful to developing countries when it does the following.

✗ The aid reaches the government but not those who need it.

✗ The aid is given for selfish reasons to please the donor country.

✗ The aid encourages those receiving it to rely on aid and discourages a sense of personal responsibility.

✗ The aid is not designed to encourage development in the country receiving aid.

AID HAS LIMITS

As we have seen, a complex tangle of Social, Economic and Political factors can result in famine or food shortages. Even the best aid has its limits, as the causes of the problems being dealt with are so enormous and difficult to change.

● Aid cannot solve all problems. At best it can help, and encourage change.

● Aid can offer support, but on its own it cannot create the economic development needed. World prices, trade practices and financial dealings affect trade in ways which are difficult to change by aid alone.

● Loans can cause countries to sink deeper into debt and can result in those countries actually helping the rich developed countries who are giving the aid. This is achieved by paying off loans or by giving vast amounts of their natural resources and income to the donor country in repayment.

As we have seen, some types of aid are more effective than others. In Section 3, for example, we noted that the British government, through the ODA, has, as its primary objective, the goal of encouraging lasting development rather than simply reacting to a disaster and providing emergency aid. At the end of the day, good aid should result in the country receiving that aid becoming free of outside help and developing into a self-reliant economy.

TRADE – NOT AID?

A large percentage of African countries rely on one commodity for their exports and trade. African countries contribute only 4% to the annual volume of world trade but, as the following examples show, many of these countries are desperately dependent on one crop alone (see Table 1.6).

Prices for many products have slumped as figure 1.20 indicates, placing great strains on countries which have only a limited range of commodities with which to trade.

Country	Commodity	Percentage (%) of export earnings
Rwanda	Coffee	69.2
Malawi	Tobacco	64.2
Ethiopia	Coffee	50.5
Ghana	Cocoa	46.8
Burundi	Coffee	41.8
Benin	Cotton	40.5
Gambia	Ground Nuts	40.0

Table 1.6 Source: *New Internationalist*, June 1990

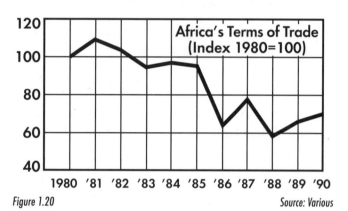

Figure 1.20 Source: Various

Figure 1.21

African countries require cash from trade to purchase imports which they cannot produce themselves. As a consequence of falling prices for the products which African countries export, it is estimated that on average they now have to sell up to 20% more just to stand still. As we saw earlier, much of the aid given to countries is tied, which often results in the donor country, rather than the recipient, benefiting.

Solutions to these problems which are based on developing trade, rather than simply giving aid, are the way forward in the view of many experts in this area. Most developing countries produce mainly *primary* products which are goods that are grown or extracted, such as bananas, coffee, rubber, copper, cotton, cocoa etc. On the other hand, developed countries rely heavily on *secondary* products which are goods which have been manufactured, such as machines, processed foods, consumer goods etc. When developing countries were controlled by European powers such as Britain, France, Portugal and the Netherlands, such African countries were known as colonies. A colony was a country which had been conquered by one of the European powers and was ruled by it.

One of the purposes of colonising African countries was to provide markets for the goods of developed countries. Thus, after gaining independence, the economies of many African countries evolved in ways which made them reliant on importing secondary products. If such countries could be relieved of the burden of having to spend millions of pounds importing products which they could produce themselves, then the massive debt owed by such countries could be reduced. For example, it is estimated that in 1987, Africa's total debt was in excess of $219 billion. The figure today is substantially higher.

Trade often works against the needs and interests of African people. As a consequence of a fall in prices for certain primary products, it is estimated that between 1980 and 1985 there was a loss to Sub-Saharan Africa of $11 billion.

Aid such as Britain's ODA contributions to Mozambique can be seen as good aid, since an attempt is being made to develop and expand trade. However, to aid developing countries in Africa truly, a massive change in the way we live in the developed North would be required. For example, as a member of the EU, Britain levies taxes and duties on many products which are imported from non-EU members. If this were to change, it could mean more unemployment in Europe in the face of a flood of cheap imports. The problems are easy to identify, but the solutions are highly complex and have far-reaching implications.

Activities

1   Make a table headed GOOD AID and BAD AID. Study the examples of aid below and decide which are examples of good aid, and which are examples of bad aid.

  - France sends long-term food aid to Gabon.

  - Britain sends advisers and teachers to Mozambique.

  - The EU organises medical training and village clinics in a number of African countries.

  - Italy grants a loan for farming research, but spending will be monitored by experts.

  - The USA grants a loan, but American produce must be bought in return.

  - International finance is given to develop tourist hotels.

2   Choose th e examples from each side of your table. Give reasons to explain why they are examples of good and bad aid.

3   Give reasons to explain why aid cannot solve the problems of African countries.

Photofile: African Images

A weaver

A Tigrayan woman

Spinning cotton

Harvesting in Tigray

What you will learn

1   How the European Union grew and developed.

2   The aims of the European Union.

3   The structure of the European Union.

THE FORMATION AND GROWTH OF THE EUROPEAN UNION

The European Union is the modern name for an organisation which started as the European Coal and Steel Community (ECSC) in 1951. The ECSC originally had six members who agreed to cooperate with regard to coal and steel production. In 1957 they signed two more treaties setting up the European Atomic Energy Commission (EURATOM) and the European Economic Community. As the Community widened its powers, the word 'Economic' was dropped from the title, and the organisation became simply the European Community. This term was changed again in the mid-1990s to the European Union.

The origins of the European Union lie in the desire of politicians in the late 1940s to avoid another war in Europe. They saw the destruction caused by two major wars and wanted to make sure that such a thing could never happen again. The key was to make the major countries of Europe—especially France and Germany—depend on each other for economic stability. This is what lay behind the formation of the European Coal and Steel Community. Two French politicians, Jean Monnet and Robert Schuman,

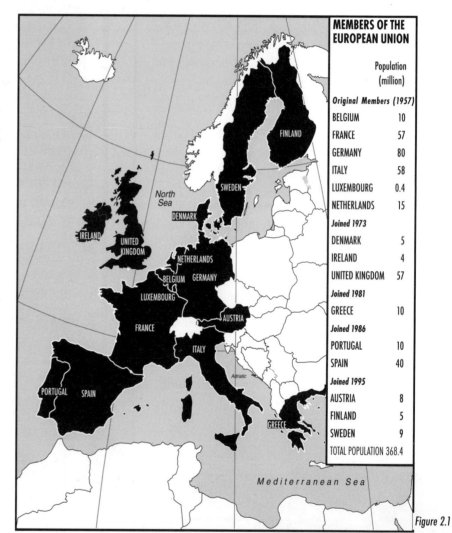

MEMBERS OF THE EUROPEAN UNION	Population (million)
Original Members (1957)	
BELGIUM	10
FRANCE	57
GERMANY	80
ITALY	58
LUXEMBOURG	0.4
NETHERLANDS	15
Joined 1973	
DENMARK	5
IRELAND	4
UNITED KINGDOM	57
Joined 1981	
GREECE	10
Joined 1986	
PORTUGAL	10
SPAIN	40
Joined 1995	
AUSTRIA	8
FINLAND	5
SWEDEN	9
TOTAL POPULATION	368.4

Figure 2.1

The European Union has a larger population than the United States of America, or the former Soviet Union, making it one of the most powerful political groupings in the world. More countries are set to join within the next ten years.

drew up the blueprint for what they called a "High Authority" to make decisions, rather than relying upon negotiations between individual governments. That 'High Authority' has grown into the European Union.

In 1957 the six members of the ECSC signed the Treaty of Rome, creating the European Economic Community. Its aim was to establish a 'Common Market' to develop and encourage trade between Community members and to improve living standards throughout all the countries of the Community.

The Treaty of Rome was basically a Customs Union. Once goods were within the Community they could be traded quite freely between countries with no taxes or duties applied. However, the Community could agree to impose taxes on goods entering from outside. In this way the member countries could protect their own industries and allow them to prosper, improving living standards within the borders of the Community.

HOW ARE DECISIONS TAKEN?

There are four main Institutions of the European Community.

The Council of Ministers still makes most of the major decisions. Every member country sends a government representative to the Council. Different Ministers attend depending on the agenda of the meeting. For example, if the Council is discussing farming then the Agriculture Minister will be sent. The Council has regular Summit Meetings when the Prime Minister of each member country attends. When there is a vote in the Council, the bigger members have more votes than the smaller members. A qualified majority voting system means that decisions have to be approved by a combination of large and small countries. If the Council wants to make major changes to the Treaties of the Union, then they can call an Inter-Governmental Conference (IGC), such as the one at Maastricht in December 1991.

The Commission is the Civil Service of the European Union. Commissioners make suggestions about policy, but their main job is to put the decisions of the Council of Ministers into practice.

The European Parliament is a directly elected assembly with delegates from all parts of the Union. They serve for a five year term, with the next elections being in mid-1999. The Parliament makes comments on draft laws and sends proposed changes to the Council of Ministers.

The European Court of Justice settles disputes about European Union law. Individual citizens can appeal to the Court if they feel that they have been unfairly treated.

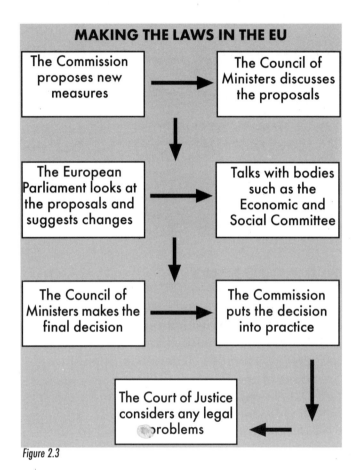

Figure 2.3

EUROPEAN PARLIAMENT COMMITTEES

The European Parliament has a total of 18 committees. These look at the various aspects of the work of the European Union, and suggest changes to laws before they are approved by the Council of Ministers.

Figure 2.2

SUMMARY OF THE AIMS OF THE EUROPEAN UNION

1 To encourage cooperation between member countries and so reduce the chance of conflict in Europe. If countries depend on each other then they cannot afford fight!

2 To improve living standards and working conditions throughout Europe.

3 To improve trade links between members, and between the European Union and the rest of the world. The Lome Convention is a treaty linking the European Union to Third World countries.

4 To even out living standards across Europe, bringing poorer areas up to the standard of the better off regions.

5 To achieve an ever closer relationship between the peoples of Europe, including freedom of movement for workers and students across the member countries.

6 Harmonisation of laws and regulations across all member countries.

Activities

1 Why did countries such as France and Germany want to form a European Union in the 1950s?

2 **"The Treaty of Rome was basically a Customs Union".** What is a Customs Union?

3 Briefly describe the powers and functions of the Council of Ministers, the Commission and the European Parliament.

4 Which part of the European Union makes the final decisions?

5 What important topics does the European Parliament debate?

6 What are the main aims of the European Union?

OBJECTIVES OF THE MAASTRICHT TREATY

★ To create a European Union of states, building on the European Community's existing provisions.

☆ To create an area without borders, where no EU members would require passports.

☯ To strengthen economic and social cooperation.

● To link the economic and financial affairs of all the EU countries.

● To create one European currency.

✦ To share a common foreign and security policy.

🚶 To introduce citizenship of the European Union.

⚖ To develop close cooperation in justice and home affairs.

MAASTRICHT

Throughout the 1970s and 1980s most of the countries in the European Community were moving towards a closer economic, monetary and political union. The so-called 'federalists', including the president of the European Commission, Jacques Delors, believed that the time had come to consolidate and deepen the ties among the existing members of the Community. They wanted to develop more common policies and more powerful Community institutions to promote and enforce them.

Out of this idea came the Maastricht Treaty—so called because it was agreed at an Inter-Governmental Conference in the Dutch town of Maastricht in December 1991.

The Maastricht Treaty then had to be ratified by each of the member governments. This meant that they had to get approval by their own Parliaments. Denmark, France and Ireland each held a referendum to ratify the Treaty, while other countries debated it in their Parliaments.

The crucial point about the Maastricht Treaty was that it extended the scope of the Community into new areas. Policies which used to be controlled by individual governments were now under the influence of Brussels.

EFFECTS OF THE TREATY

The Maastricht Treaty, when put into practice, would radically affect the way of life of all people living in the EU. Some of the consequences of the Treaty are outlined below.

a) By 1999 the currencies of the EU members should be replaced by a Single European Currency, the Euro. A new European Central Bank will be set up, taking over the role of individual Central Banks like the Bank of England.

b) All citizens of member countries become citizens of the European Union.

c) The Social Chapter aims to harmonise laws about working conditions throughout the EU.

Workers should have the same rights in every country. Britain has opted out of this part of the Treaty.

d) Greater cooperation on justice and home affairs, such as drugs, refugees, terrorism and crime.

e) Greater cooperation on defence, with a growing role for the Western European Union (WEU). This can be seen as an EU defence organisation, or as the European arm of NATO.

f) Greater powers for the European Parliament and the Council of Ministers in order to reduce the influence of the Commission.

g) A new £12 billion Cohesion Fund to improve the Regional Policy.

Britain has been less enthusiastic than most countries about the Maastricht Treaty, and has opted out of provisions such as the Social Chapter. (See page 39 'the Eurosceptics')

CRITICISMS OF THE TREATY

There was considerable criticism of the Maastricht Treaty in Britain with a large section of the Conservative Party opposed to it. The criticisms which were made are summarised below.

● Individual countries lose power as power is switched from national governments to the EU.

● Too much power is given to the EU institutions, which are undemocratic in the first place.

● Unacceptable common laws are imposed over a huge area. They cannot take account of the different cultures, traditions and peoples living in these areas.

● Social Chapter will force businesses to close or move out of Europe because of high costs. Manufacturing may desert Europe totally and move to the Far East.

● Poorer regions will lose out from the European Monetary Union. With one currency wealth will be even more concentrated in the prosperous areas of the EU. It will remove one of the trading advantages which poorer countries have.

Activities

1　Why are the objectives of the Maastricht Treaty likely to cause disagreement amongst EU countries?

2　What aspect of the Maastricht Treaty did the British government refuse to accept?

3　Why do you think the British government rejected this part of the Treaty?

4　Study the sources below and answer the question which follows.

Source 1

"Britain joined the European Community in 1973 after several unsuccessful attempts to join before that. Looking back, people should realise what an important step this was. Britain has been able to join with its European neighbours to play a full part in the Community. Britain has benefited greatly from membership and will continue to do so in the future.

Hopefully Britain will eventually come into line with its European partners concerning the Social Chapter of the Maastricht Treaty."

View of a Liberal Democrat MP

Source 2

"The French tried to stop Britain joining the European Community, and they succeeded twice in the 1960s. However, Britain eventually did join in 1973 and that decision has proved to be a bad one. Britain has had to accept all sorts of decisions from Europe which we did not want. Thankfully we were able to opt out of the Social Chapter of the Maastricht Treaty which must be one of the worst pieces of European legislation ever. Britain must be able to make up its own mind about important issues." *View of a Conservative MP*

Sources 1 and 2 give different views about Britain's membership of the European Community.

Using your own words say what these differences are. Mention at least two differences.

THE SINGLE EUROPEAN MARKET
Benefits of EU Membership

What you will learn

The reasons why countries have joined and more want to join the EU:

Trade Opportunities;

Access to EU Funds;

Agricultural Policy.

A SINGLE EUROPEAN MARKET

The idea of creating a 'common market' dates back to the beginnings of the European Union in the Treaty of Rome. The aim of the Single Market is to create an area in which goods, money, people and services can circulate freely without the restrictions of frontiers, subject to certain essential safeguards.

In the past, countries used to impose taxes and duties on imports. This was done to make their own goods cheaper than those from other countries which would, therefore, protect their own industries. Members of the European Union have agreed not to charge any duties or taxes on goods traded between members. They have also agreed common levels of duty to charge on certain goods entering the Union.

This agreement has increased competition within the European Union, meaning that people should get better value, choice and quality.

Citizens of all European Union countries are now entitled to live and work in any other member state. In the past this was difficult because of different laws in the various countries. Now people have full entitlement to social security payments, benefits, medical care and education regardless of which European Union country they choose to live in. Efforts are being made to recognise educational qualifications in other European countries. Your Standard Grade qualifications should soon be recognised and valued in France, Germany and so on.

The idea of setting up the Single European Market was agreed by the Council of Ministers in 1985. They set themselves the target of completing the Single European Market by the end of 1992. This was duly achieved.

HARMONISATION

Over 300 new laws have been passed as part of the completion of the Single European Market. These cover areas such as Trading Standards and Food Laws. Toys sold in the European Union should now carry the letters CE to show they have met European safety standards. Food needs to list all the ingredients on the packaging. Even your school mini-bus has been affected by EU laws—it now has to have yellow warning plates at the front and back to show that it carries children and young people.

Memo

HIGHLAND FOUNTAIN
Mineral Waters from Scotland

From: Managing Director

To: Sales Director

As Britain is now part of the Single European Market, I suggest that we expand our sales force and employ new salespeople and representatives in the following European locations:

Frankfurt   Athens   Lyon   Vienna

Florence   Stockholm   Madrid   Antwerp

Our market research shows that there is demand for Scottish Mineral Water throughout Europe. It is up to us to fill the gap in the market and increase our sales.

Figure 2.4

TRADE OPPORTUNITIES

Scottish businesses now have the chance to sell their products throughout the European Union. There are more than 350 million potential customers out there who might buy Scottish goods.

Of course, just as Scottish companies have the opportunity to expand into the European market, businesses in Germany, France and the other member states can now sell their goods in Scotland without any restriction.

Highland Fountain Mineral Water would have to produce a very good product to compete with the well-known brands from continental Europe.

THE COMMON AGRICULTURAL POLICY

The Common Agricultural Policy has been the cause of a great deal of controversy in Britain. Many politicians, and indeed ordinary people, in this country see the Common Agricultural Policy (CAP) as one of the major problems of the European Union. It takes up more than half of the entire budget of the EU and often leads to bitter disputes between member countries.

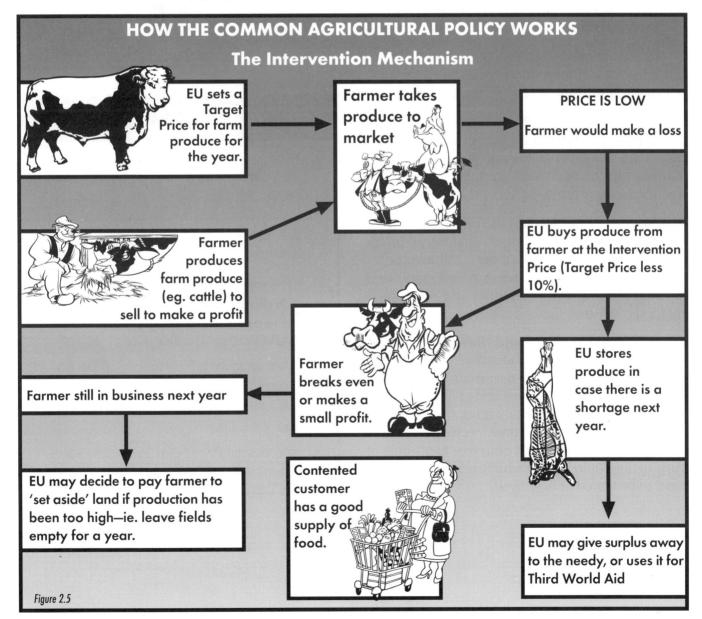

HOW THE COMMON AGRICULTURAL POLICY WORKS

The Intervention Mechanism

EU sets a Target Price for farm produce for the year.

Farmer takes produce to market

PRICE IS LOW
Farmer would make a loss

Farmer produces farm produce (eg. cattle) to sell to make a profit

EU buys produce from farmer at the Intervention Price (Target Price less 10%).

Farmer breaks even or makes a small profit.

Farmer still in business next year

EU stores produce in case there is a shortage next year.

EU may decide to pay farmer to 'set aside' land if production has been too high—ie. leave fields empty for a year.

Contented customer has a good supply of food.

EU may give surplus away to the needy, or uses it for Third World Aid

Figure 2.5

However, Britain's situation is different from most other European Union member countries. Only a very small proportion of our work force is employed in agriculture. Although farming is very important in some areas of Britain, farmers themselves are not a large and powerful group in the country. The same is not true in France, for example, where agriculture employs a comparatively large proportion of workers and farmers are a very powerful and influential pressure group.

The Common Agricultural Policy has a number of aims. These include:

⚑ ensuring a reasonable level of income for the farming community;

⚑ bringing agricultural prices together at the same level across the EU;

⚑ preventing any one member state gaining an advantage in production due to cheap labour costs;

⚑ ensuring steady supplies of all main food products, and therefore making sure that prices remain stable;

⚑ improving the productivity of farms through modern technology and methods.

Ordinary people in the United Kingdom have benefited from the CAP in a number of ways. Food prices are relatively stable and there are seldom shortages of the main food products. Also, there is a wider choice of products from other EU countries.

The farming community has also benefited from the CAP. Firstly, it has given farmers guaranteed prices for products which means a more stable income for them. Secondly, the CAP has provided grants and subsidies to improve equipment and production methods on farms

Despite these benefits, people have criticised the CAP for leading to 'overproduction'. The EU is responsible for large 'food mountains' of surplus products such as butter, beef and grain. These surpluses are the result of guaranteeing prices to farmers. However, from time to time less well-off people throughout the EU benefit from free hand-outs of surplus beef and butter which would otherwise need to be stored or destroyed.

The CAP claimed to guarantee reliable supplies of a wide range of products.

The CAP also produced surplus food which was often destroyed.

Activities

1 Why do some people feel that the Common Agricultural Policy is one of the biggest problems of the EU?

2 Why do people in France tend to feel differently about the CAP compared to people in Britain?

3 What are the aims of the CAP?

4 **"Ordinary people in Scotland have no reason to be happy with the CAP."**

   What evidence is there to suggest that this statement is biased or exaggerated?

5 Why are farmers usually happy with the way the CAP works?

6 Why are shop customers also usually happy with the way the CAP works?

AID TO THE REGIONS

Scotland benefits from the fact that the European Union distributes money to the comparatively poor regions of Europe. Studies are done to establish which areas in every EU country have average incomes which are lower than the average for the whole European Union. Once these areas have been identified they are targetted for special help.

In the language of the European Union, there are five objectives (reasons) for helping areas.

Objective	Fund
1 to assist regions whose development is lagging behind	ERDF
2 to renew regions affected by serious industrial decline	ERDF
3 to tackle long-term unemployment	ESF
4 to provide work for young people	ESF
5 to develop rural areas	EAGGF
(ERDF = European Regional Development Fund *ESF = European Social Fund* *EAGGF = European Agricultural Guidance and Guarantee Fund)*	

These funds are known as the European Structural Funds. The European Regional Development Fund is the biggest source of money for Scotland.

The Highlands and Islands of Scotland qualify for help under Objective 1. Average incomes in the Highlands are lower than 75% of the European Union average. Much of Central Scotland qualifies for help under Objective 2. Old established traditional industries such as coal mining, iron and steel and shipbuilding have declined in the last thirty years and now employ very few people indeed. The rest of Scotland qualifies for smaller amounts of assistance through Objectives 3 and 4.

From time to time the EU introduces special programmes with limited lifespans. One such initiative was the RECHAR programme, which provided funds to areas affected by the decline in coal mining. This project ended in 1993, but many areas of Central Scotland benefited from it.

The European Union will not give direct financial help to businesses. Instead, they will co-fund projects along with the government and local councils to improve the conditions in an area, making it more attractive for businesses to set up there. The theory is that if businesses can be attracted into a depressed area, then this will create jobs, raise income levels and contribute to a higher standard of living throughout the area.

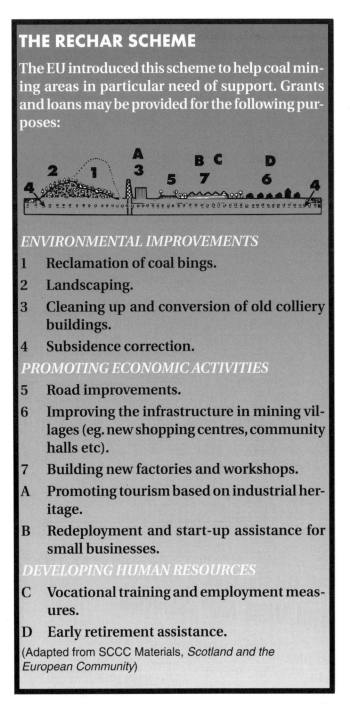

THE RECHAR SCHEME

The EU introduced this scheme to help coal mining areas in particular need of support. Grants and loans may be provided for the following purposes:

ENVIRONMENTAL IMPROVEMENTS

1 Reclamation of coal bings.

2 Landscaping.

3 Cleaning up and conversion of old colliery buildings.

4 Subsidence correction.

PROMOTING ECONOMIC ACTIVITIES

5 Road improvements.

6 Improving the infrastructure in mining villages (eg. new shopping centres, community halls etc).

7 Building new factories and workshops.

A Promoting tourism based on industrial heritage.

B Redeployment and start-up assistance for small businesses.

DEVELOPING HUMAN RESOURCES

C Vocational training and employment measures.

D Early retirement assistance.

(Adapted from SCCC Materials, *Scotland and the European Community*)

European Union aid to the regions is based on three principles. The first of these is partnership. There must be involvement from national governments and local councils, as well as from the EU itself. The second principle is subsidiarity. The EU believes that decisions should be made at the local level to ensure that the best use is made of the funds available. The third principle is additionality. This means that EU money must be used in addition to, rather than instead of, money from within the country concerned.

When applying for funds it is normally local councils who prepare the submission. They must make sure that their plans match up with one of the five Objectives and will lead to improved living standards. The EU may provide up to 50% of the cost for certain projects.

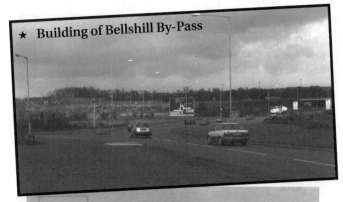

★ Building of Bellshill By-Pass

EXAMPLES OF PROJECTS FUNDED BY EU AID

- ★ Ferry Services to Western Isles
- ☆ Causeway from Barra to Vatersay
- ★ Improvements to Inverness Airport
- ☆ Improvements to Tiree Airstrip
- ★ Electrification of Glasgow-Largs Railway
- ☆ Heightening of Carron Dam, creating a larger reservoir serving Central Region
- ★ Dundee Sewer Project
- ☆ New bird observatory on Fair Isle
- ★ Pedestrianisation of Alloa Town Centre
- ☆ New Industrial / Business Park and retail development at Forthbank, Stirling

NEW OBJECTIVE 1 STATUS FOR THE HIGHLANDS AND ISLANDS

Incomes in the Highlands and Islands are less than 75% of the EU average, so the area now qualifies for Objective 1 help. This opens up vast funds for use and may lead to many new projects in the area. It is hoped to establish a University in the Highlands and to make further improvements to the road network. The EU has already given considerable help to tourist related developments in the Highlands and Islands.

AID TO THE HIGHLANDS AND ISLANDS, 1988–1993

Total £156 million (of which £76 million came from the EU)

Transport Improvements	– £89 million
Business support	– £24 million
Tourism	– £8 million
Electricity, water and sewage	– £32 million
Training facilities	– £3 million

PROJECTS SUPPORTED BY THE EU
1992–'93

Central Region

Source of Finance: £12 million from ERDF
£20 million from local and national government
£5 million from private funds.

Projects: Industrial units at Stirling, Springkerse and Grangemouth; pedestrianisation of Stirling and Grangemouth town centres; re-opening of Camelon Railway station, and improvements to the road network.

Fife Region

Source of Finance: £14 million from ERDF
£22 million from local and national government
£6 million from private funds.

Projects: New units for small businesses at North Queensferry, Dunfermline and Kirkcaldy; improvements to the road and rail network, coastal protection at East Wemyss, improvements to Cowdenbeath and Glenrothes town centres, and tourist developments such as the Fife Coastal Footpath.

★ Tourism and Leisure Centre at Coatbridge

Activities

1. Why does Scotland receive help from the EU Structural Funds?
2. Which areas of Scotland are given the most help by the EU?
3. What was the purpose of the RECHAR scheme?
4. Explain the three principles upon which European Union aid is based.
5. Look at the examples of projects supported by EU aid throughout Scotland. Choose at least five of them and explain exactly why the EU will support those particular projects. What benefits will they bring to their areas?

TRADE AND THE EUROPEAN UNION

THE LOMÉ CONVENTION

The countries of the European Union produce most of the goods that they require. However, there are some products which they need to import. These include many primary products such as minerals, raw materials and agricultural products.

Countries such as France, Britain, Spain and Italy were all important colonial powers in the past. Their empires covered large parts of Africa, Latin America and the Pacific Islands. Because of this they still have many strong ties with these parts of the world.

The Lomé Convention is an agreement between the European Union nations and the African, Caribbean and Pacific (ACP) countries. The Convention helps both sides. The ACP countries can export their produce to Europe without restriction, giving Europe access to supplies of things which it cannot produce for itself. The European Union supports development projects in the ACP countries through non-repayable aid.

European Union countries can also export manufactured goods to the ACP nations thus boosting industry in Europe. This could become even more important if EU aid to the ACP countries leads to a long-term rise in their living standards and increases their purchasing power.

THE EU AND EASTERN EUROPE

Many of the nations of Eastern Europe would like to join the European Union, but this is unlikely to happen until at least the year 2000. (see page 38) However, the EU still has a role to play in the economic development of Eastern Europe.

The EU is spending large amounts of money in Eastern Europe. The *Phare* scheme gives technical aid to Eastern Europe, while the *Tacis* scheme helps the former Soviet Union. In 1993 Phare assistance totalled £800 million and Tacis aid came to £390 million.

The money is used to pay western experts to advise on economic development. Sometimes this deals with privatisation of old state-run industries; sometimes it may deal with clearing up environmental problems. In Hungary, Phare aid was used to establish a stock exchange system and to privatise departments in the civil service.

If the former Communist countries are ever to be able to join the EU, then their industries and businesses need to modernise very quickly. They will have no chance in a competitive market against the industrial giants of Western Europe if this does not happen.

EUROPEAN COMMUNITY TRADE (1989)		
Trading Partner	Exports(%)	Imports(%)
EFTA	25.9	22.8
USA	18.8	18.7
Japan	5.0	10.3
Latin America	3.6	5.8
ACP Countries	3.4	4.4
Former USSR	2.9	3.4

EFTA - European Free Trade Association, included Austria, Switzerland, Iceland, Sweden, Norway, Finland

ACP - African, Caribbean and Pacific countries with links to EU through the Lomé Convention

Table 2.1

Activities

1 Table 2.1 is obviously now out of date. What will have happened to the European Community trade with EFTA countries since 1989?

   (Clue – think of what will have happened since 1 January 1995).

2 What are the aims of the Lomé Convention?

3 *"The Lomé Convention only helps European countries. It does nothing to help the situation in countries in the Third World"*.

   Give evidence to suggest that this statement is an example of selective use of facts .

4 What are the aims of the Phare and Tacis schemes?

5 What benefit could there be for EU countries if the economies of eastern European countries were to develop quickly?

6 What evidence can you find of EU aid for projects in your own home area?

CONDITIONS FOR EU MEMBERSHIP

Any country which wants to join the European Union must satisfy a number of conditions. It must be a European country with a democratic government which respects human rights.

The EU now also insists that the economy of any applicant country must be strong enough and developed enough to allow it to compete on equal terms with the established members.

FURTHER ENLARGEMENT OF THE EUROPEAN UNION

Austria, Finland and Sweden joined the European Union on 1 January 1995, bringing the total membership up to fifteen countries. Norway would have joined as well, but the people voted against the move in a national referendum.

Other countries have applied to join the EU. Cyprus, Malta and Turkey had applications on the table in mid-1995. Cyprus is unlikely to be admitted because of the political split on the island between Greek and Turkish factions, while Turkey is likely to be rejected because its economy is less developed than that of the EU members.

The major debate centres on the

POTENTIAL MEMBERS OF THE EUROPEAN UNION

STRUGGLING ECONOMIES	POLITICALLY UNSTABLE
Turkey	Cyprus
Slovakia	Croatia
Albania	Bosnia
Romania	Serbia
Bulgaria	

WIDENING v DEEPENING

At present there is a debate within the EU over whether its role should be widened or deepened. Widening means admitting more members; deepening means increasing the powers of the EU within the existing membership.

European Union Members

Countries who wish to join the European Union

Figure 2.6

Eastern European countries of the former Soviet bloc. Poland, the Czech Republic, Hungary, Slovakia, Bulgaria, Romania and Albania are all eager to join the EU. Only Poland, the Czech Republic and Hungary could realistically become members before the end of the century.

However, by the mid-'90s the EU was reluctant to admit Eastern European countries. The arguments in favour of accepting these countries seemed to be outweighed by the arguments against.

In favour of accepting the Eastern

European countries was the fact that it would open a new market for exports. There would be a large demand in the Eastern European countries for good quality products from countries such as Britain. It would also strengthen the European ideal of a united Europe living in peace.

However, the arguments against were very strong. Firstly, it was argued that increasing the membership to these countries would open the barriers to migration. Many Eastern European people might move to Western Europe, looking for work and expecting a higher living standard.

Secondly, low wages in the east could encourage firms to move there, causing unemployment in the west.

Finally, it would be very expensive for the European Regional Development Fund and the Common Agricultural Policy.

THE EUROSCEPTICS

Some people in Britain would prefer the country to leave the European Union. This issue has caused disagreements within the Conservative Party which is split over its attitude towards Europe. People opposed to Britain's membership of the European Union are called Eurosceptics. They put forward several arguments to back their view.

● Loss of Sovereignty

Britain has to give up power to the European Union, and fewer decisions are made at Westminster than before. Some people resent giving up power to Brussels.

● *Britain's 'Special Relationship' with America*

Britain has had long-established links with the USA, which would be weakened if we integrated more with Europe. Britain also has traditional links with the Commonwealth countries such as Australia, Canada and New Zealand.

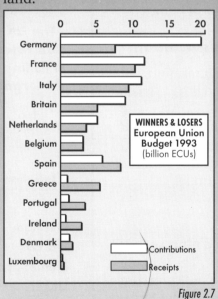

Figure 2.7

● Cost

Britain's contributions to the EU budget are considerable. Some people believe that we do not get as much back as other countries because we are not a major agricultural nation.

What has happened in recent years is that countries such as Britain have been able to 'opt out' of particular pieces of European legislation which they do not like. In Britain's case this included the 'social chapter' of the Maastricht Treaty, also known as the 'Social Charter'.

Conservative politicians felt that this was more like Labour Party policy, with sections on minimum wages, working conditions, maternity rights and so on. In order that the Maastricht Bill would not be defeated in the House of Commons, the European Union allowed Britain to 'opt out' of this part of the Treaty while accepting the other terms of the Maastricht Agreement. This meant that the Social Charter became a non-binding 'Protocol' rather than an integral part of the Maastricht Treaty itself.

Anti-Europeans saw it as vital that the Social Chapter was removed from the Bill. If this had not been done, they said, British industry would have become less competitive leading to higher unemployment and the failure of many businesses.

Many people within the Conservative Party argue that the UK membership of the European Union should be decided by a referendum of the British people. The last time that this happened, in 1975, the electorate voted to remain part of the organisation we had joined in 1973.

OTHER EUROPEAN ECONOMIC ORGANISATIONS

The European Union is not the only Economic Alliance serving the needs of the nations of Europe.

EFTA – European Free Trade Association

This used to be a more important organisation, but most of its members have now joined the EU itself, leaving only Iceland, Liechtenstein, Norway and Switzerland as full members. EFTA has negotiated free-trade agreements between its members and EU countries, and has also forged close links with the emerging democracies of Eastern Europe.

COUNCIL OF EUROPE

This has thirty two full members and nine 'special guest' members from Eastern Europe. The Council of Europe is especially interested in cultural and heritage matters, and it also established the European Convention on Human Rights.

EUROPEAN BANK FOR RECONSTRUCTION AND DEVELOPMENT

Started in 1991, the aim of the EBRD is to assist the transformation of the states of Eastern and Central Europe from centrally-planned communist economies to full market economies.

ORGANISATION FOR ECONOMIC COOPERATION AND DEVELOPMENT

The OECD includes the main countries of Europe, plus Australia, Canada, New Zealand and Mexico. It tries to coordinate economic policy to create sound economic growth around the world.

WESTERN EUROPEAN UNION

The WEU has developed a role as the military and defence branch of the European Union. This role has expanded in the 1990s as the United States has lessened its commitment to NATO, creating a need for a strong European defence agency.

Countries join these alliances for the same reasons as they join or seek to join the European Union itself. They see benefits from membership, and support the ideals of European unity and cooperation.

1   The reasons why NATO was formed.

2   How NATO has grown since the 1940s.

3   The role of NATO during the Cold War.

THE ORIGINS AND FORMATION OF NATO

During World War Two Britain, the United States of America and the Soviet Union fought together against the common enemy of Nazi Germany. However, as the war went on, the relationship between the 'Allies' became more and more uneasy. In particular, Britain and America began to mistrust the Soviet Union.

At the end of the War the Soviet Union had freed most of Eastern and Central Europe from German control. The Allies argued over which of them should 'occupy' the liberated areas, and the uneasy relationship between them became a deep split.

The Soviet Union went its own way. It had a different ideology and used its power to dominate Eastern Europe.

Britain, the United States, Canada and the liberated countries of Western Europe decided to join together to form the North Atlantic Treaty Organisation (NATO). NATO was established in April 1949. The main aim of the organisation was to protect Western Europe from any further expansion by the Soviet Union. Eastern Europe had come under Moscow's control and communist governments had been established in what were now known as the 'satellite states' of the USSR.

NATO aimed to keep the peace in Europe through a Collective Defence policy. The idea was that if any NATO member was attacked, then this would be seen as an attack on the whole organisation.

THE NORTH ATLANTIC TREATY ORGANISATION AND THE DIVISION OF EUROPE

Europe was divided by the Iron Curtain after 1945. The USSR dominated Eastern Europe and NATO was formed in Western Europe along with Canada and the USA.

NATO MEMBERSHIP

Original Members (1949):

Belgium	Luxembourg
Canada	Netherlands
Denmark	Norway
France	Portugal
Iceland	United Kingdom
Italy	United States

Later members:
West Germany (1955)
Greece (1952)
Spain (1982)
Turkey (1952)

KEY   N=Netherlands   B=Belgium   ▨ Members of NATO   〜 Iron Curtain

Figure 3.1

After 1949 there was no further expansion of Communism and no major wars have been fought in Europe. Therefore it can be argued that NATO has been a major success.

HOW NATO WORKS

NATO has been able to ensure that the military forces and defence policies of the member countries have been planned and organised in a cooperative way.

The member countries had the shared aim of trying to prevent any further expansion of Communism, and they put this into practice through military cooperation. The Western European countries might not have been able to put together such a strong military alliance on their own, therefore the presence of the United States was vital.

All NATO forces come under the command of Allied Command Europe (ACE) which was set up to defend Europe—from the Arctic in the North to the Mediterranean in the South—from the possible threat of Soviet invasion. NATO built up a huge store of conventional and nuclear weapons. They carried out regular military exercises and intensive training programmes to make sure they would be ready if the attack ever came.

NATO's top decision making body is the Council, made up of politicians from all the member countries. Military planning and training is the responsibility of the Military Committee, formed by the Chief of Defence Staffs from each country. NATO's main offices are in Brussels, and the military headquarters, the Supreme Headquarters Allied Powers Europe (SHAPE), are nearby at Mons.

FACTFILE: The Cold war

How the Cold War was fought by the USA and the USSR

● **Propaganda**: Each side produced propaganda about the other. Much of this was exaggerated; some was outright lies. Propaganda was broadcast on radio and published in print.

● **Wars:** Both the USA and the USSR gave arms and military advice to many countries in Africa, Asia and Latin America. When wars broke out in these parts of the world, one side was usually American backed and the other Soviet backed. Sometimes they sent troops to fight, but never directly with each other. Examples of these wars included the conflicts in Vietnam and the Middle East.

● **Aid:** To try and win influence in other countries, both the superpowers provided economic and humanitarian aid to poorer countries.

● **Space:** The Space Race was fought out between the USA and the USSR. The USSR launched the first satellites and put the first man in space. The USA was the first to put men on the moon.

● **The Arms Race:** This was the most alarming part of the Cold War, as the superpowers competed to produce the largest and most dangerous weapons. Both of them had huge stores of conventional and nuclear weapons with which they could have brought total devastation to the planet. The theory of Mutually Assured Destruction meant that neither side would start a war because they knew that their opponents were so powerful that they could not possibly win—both sides would be destroyed. However, the presence of thousands of nuclear weapons made the world a very dangerous place.

● **Sport & Culture:** In the Olympic Games the superpowers competed to see who could win the most medals. This brought great prestige to their country.

The USSR was especially keen to build up a reputation as a cultural nation with huge government support for the State Theatre, Opera, Ballet and Circus.

● **Threats & Warnings:** The superpowers frequently issued threats, warnings and ultimatums. In 1962 the Soviet Union tried to establish missile bases on Cuba,  less than a hundred miles from the USA. President Kennedy threatened to take military action against the USSR and issued an ultimatum demanding that no missiles should be based on Cuba. The government in Moscow backed down, preventing a situation developing which could have led to nuclear war between the superpowers.

FACTFILE: Berlin

France and the USA also controlled a sector of the city.

1948 – The Soviet Union cut off West Berlin from the UK, French and American zones of Germany. They were trying to force the western allies out of Berlin by a blockade. The Berlin Airlift was mounted to beat the blockade and for nearly a year all supplies had to be flown into West Berlin.

1949 – The French, British and American zones of Germany became the Federal Republic of Germany (West Germany), and the Soviet Zone became the German Democratic Republic (East Germany).

1961 – East Germany and East Berlin were sealed off by the building of the Berlin Wall. People trying to escape from East Germany to the West were arrested or shot. President Kennedy visited the city and made it clear that America and NATO would not give up West Berlin.

1970s – Attempts were made to develop more links between East and West Germany through Willy Brandt's Ostpolitik, but very little progress was made.

1989 – Reforms in other parts of Eastern Europe meant that East Germans could escape via Hungary and Austria to the West. The East German government opened up the Berlin Wall and paved the way for the reunification of Germany.

1945 – Soviet forces entered Berlin. Hitler killed himself. At the Potsdam Conference the Allies agreed to divide Germany into four zones of occupation. Berlin was within the Soviet zone, but each of Britain,

British Zone

Berlin

EAST GERMANY

WEST GERMANY

Russian Zone

French Zone

US Zone

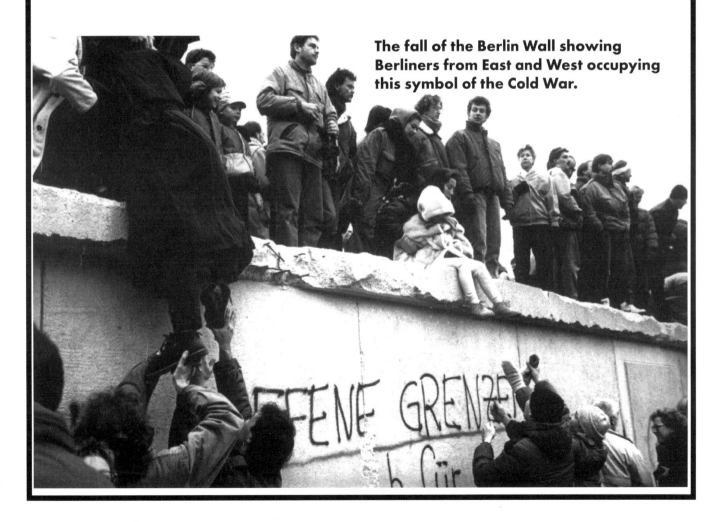

The fall of the Berlin Wall showing Berliners from East and West occupying this symbol of the Cold War.

BACKGROUND TO THE COLD WAR

From 1945 until the late 1980s, the USA and the USSR opposed each other in what was known as the Cold War. They never took part in direct armed conflict with each other, but at times the world was close to a war between the two superpowers.

Why did the USA and the USSR hate each other so much? The answer lies in the different *ideologies* of each country.

The ideology in the United States of America was *capitalism*. The USA had a history of democracy and human rights, and under the capitalist economic system people had great individual freedom to live and work as they wanted to. Many people were able to become rich and enjoy great personal wealth.

In the USSR the ideology was *communism*. Under this system the government controlled most aspects of people's lives. There was little individual freedom and no regular elections which could change the government. People were not allowed to leave the country without government approval.

Both countries were convinced that their ideology was the best one. Each was frightened that the other superpower would try and expand its influence over a wider area. Therefore, to try and prevent any spread of a hated ideology, the superpowers built up alliances to strengthen their positions.

NATO played a big part in the Cold War since it was the military alliance between the United States and the major Western European nations, who were concerned by the threat from Moscow.

Activities

1 When and why was NATO established?

2 Why is it accurate to describe NATO as 'The Atlantic Alliance'?

3 Why was the presence of the USA vital to NATO?

4 Briefly describe the ideologies of the USA and the USSR during the Cold War years.

5 What was 'The Cold War'?

6 Write a short essay on the ways in which the Cold War was fought. Try to use examples of your own to illustrate the various points.

WHY DID THE COLD WAR END?

Throughout the 1960s, '70s and early '80s attempts were made by the leaders of the USA and the USSR to reach agreements on Arms Control and to limit the development of new weapons. Despite some agreements the picture still looked bad in the early 1980s with developments such as Cruise Missiles, SS20s and the American Strategic Defence Initiative (Star Wars).

President Reagan, elected in 1980, seemed to be taking a very hard line in dealings with Moscow, and the Soviet leaders of the time were part of the old-fashioned Communist tradition. There seemed to be little hope of progress.

This all changed when the Soviet Union chose Mikhail Gorbachev as its new leader in 1985. He represented a new generation of Communists and he was quick to seek change. In his own country he developed the policies of 'glasnost' and 'perestroika', making government more open and accountable and trying to modernise the economy.

Within a couple of years it was clear that Gorbachev was concerned mainly with trying to improve the situation within the USSR and was not really bothered about fighting a 'Cold War' with the outside world. Agreements were reached to reduce arms and destroy whole classes of weapons. The countries of Eastern Europe began to change. If any of them had shown defiance against Moscow in the 1950s and '60s, they would have been invaded; in the late 1980s Gorbachev actually encouraged them to change.

Mikhail Gorbachev

A series of revolutions swept across Eastern Europe as the Communists were removed from power and democratic elections were held. In Poland, Czechoslovakia, Bulgaria, Albania, Hungary and East Germany this happened relatively peacefully, but in Romania there was a brief period of fighting before the Communists were overthrown.

The ideological division which had split Europe was removed. Germany was reunified and the old links between East and West were re-established across Europe.

Gorbachev had hoped to keep the Soviet Union together as one country, and he had wanted to reform the economy and improve living standards. However, he was unable to do so. Various parts of the old Soviet Union broke away and became independent, including some of the nations of the 'New Europe'—Lithuania, Estonia, Latvia, Belarus, Ukraine etc.

Boris Yeltsin

Opponents of Gorbachev criticised him for not making changes quickly enough and he was replaced as leader in Moscow by Boris Yeltsin.

However, Gorbachev will always be remembered as the politician who was brave enough to bring the Cold War to a end and lay the foundations for a more peaceful Europe.

THE NEW GERMANY

The end of the Cold War had a particularly significant effect on Germany. The country which had been divided at the end of the Second World War was reunited. During the Cold War the Iron Curtain had divided Germany into two countries, each with its own ideology. The Berlin Wall surrounded the western section of Germany's capital city, creating an island of capitalism inside the communist German Democratic Republic.

The end of the Cold War brought this division to an end. Communities which had been divided by the border were reunited as Germany became one country again. However, reunification highlighted the differences in wealth which existed between the two parts of the country. The West had prospered under the capitalist system and the people there enjoyed a living standard far beyond that of their counterparts in the East.

Industries in the East had little chance of surviving against competition from the West. The new technology and modern production and management methods used in the West gave them a great advantage. The result of this was unemployment in the former German Democratic Republic.

Activities

1 **"Berlin was the focus of some of the most dangerous events of the Cold War. The world was brought to the brink of war because of events in Berlin."**

What evidence is there to support this statement?

2 **"The border between East and West Germany has to be secure so that the capitalist influences of the West do not affect our land."**
(East German spokesperson)

"The heavily defended border exists purely to prevent East German people from escaping to the West."
(West German spokesperson)

Which of the two views do you support? Give reasons to back up your answer.

3 What changes did Gorbachev make in the USSR which led to the end of the Cold War?

4 How did Gorbachev treat the Eastern European countries compared to previous Soviet leaders?

5 Why was Gorbachev replaced as leader by Boris Yeltsin?

6 In what ways does membership of NATO help to meet the modern defence needs of countries like Britain?

This led to some social unrest in the East with violence flaring against minority groups in cities such as Rostock. The economy of the West also suffered as the German government tried to subsidise the poorer areas in the East. Taxation rose and prosperity fell as reunification led to a move towards equalisation of the two parts of Germany.

However, the new Germany is still the most powerful economic force in Europe. With a population of over 70 million and an economy which is still one of the most successful on the continent, Germany has a major role to play in the future of Europe.

CHAPTER

3

MILITARY ALLIANCES IN EUROPE – SECTION 2

NATO TODAY

What you will learn

1 The arguments for and against retaining NATO in the late 1990s.

2 What the current problems are within NATO.

3 The changing role of NATO in the 1990s.

DO WE STILL NEED NATO?

NATO was formed to challenge the threat which the USSR posed for countries in Western Europe. With the collapse of the USSR, many people see no point in NATO continuing to exist.

Throughout the 1960s, '70s and '80s NATO countries armed themselves with highly sophisticated, but extremely expensive, weapons systems. The phrase 'the peace dividend' is used to describe the opportunity which exists to save the huge amount of money that used to be spent on the development and manufacture of weapons.

ARGUMENTS FOR RETAINING NATO

● The former Soviet Union is still very unstable. There are extremists who would like to follow Boris Yeltsin as leader of Russia. Wars are being fought in areas such as Chechenya, Armenia and Georgia. There could still be a military threat from this area.

● There are other conflicts in Europe such as the war in Bosnia and other parts of the former Yugoslavia. If NATO stays together then it is less likely that other countries could be drawn into this conflict. NATO could also act as a 'police force' to keep the peace in areas of conflict.

● Leaders such as Saddam Hussein (Iraq) and Colonel Gaddaffi (Libya) have been a threat to the developed world in recent years. If NATO remains as a united force, then these leaders and others like them would be less able to exert influence over world events.

● The consequences of dismantling NATO would be very expensive economically. Thouands of American troops are stationed in Europe and thousands of people are employed in the arms and defence-related industries around the world.

● NATO has kept the peace effectively since the end of World War Two. There have been fifty years of peace with NATO around—why risk changing this?

Who needs NATO?

ARGUMENTS FOR ENDING NATO

● NATO was established to guard against the spread of Communism from the former Soviet Union. The USA also set up similar organisations in Central Asia (CENTO) and South East Asia (SEATO). Now that the Communist government has gone from the Soviet Union, there is no reason for retaining NATO.

● The Cold War is over. The great ideological differences between East and West no longer exist. Europe is becoming a much more united place. The idea of a defence force, based on ideology, is out of date.

● European countries should have their own Alliance without relying on the United States of America. For nearly fifty years America was prepared to fight a war on European soil. American troops should go now and leave Europe to run its own affairs.

● The money spent on weapons and defence could be better spent on other things. In Britain the health service, education, transport and welfare could all benefit from some of the money which has previously been spent on arms.

● America is concerned that its contribution to the costs of NATO is by far the greatest. Within the United States there is a growing feeling that Europe should be left to look after its own defence matters.

NATO'S CHANGING ROLE

In 1990 NATO heads of state and government changed the goals and policies of the organisation following the end of the Cold War. They issued a *Declaration of Peace and Cooperation* in 1991, and announced cutbacks of around 30% in troops and weapons.

The main points of the new strategy included:

- Less dependence on nuclear weapons. NATO is less likely to be involved in a major superpower conflict than before.

- More flexible forces, able to undertake a variety of tasks. In the past, NATO forces had expected an attack from the East and nothing else.

- Greater use of multinational forces. Before, NATO was organised along the lines of cooperation between national armies; now forces will be made up of troops from a number of different countries.

- Active involvement in international peacekeeping forces.

- More cooperation with other international organisations.

The North Atlantic Cooperation Council was also set up to bring the NATO members closer to the countries of Eastern Europe and the former Soviet Union. Some of the former Communist countries would now like to join NATO itself.

In January 1994, NATO launched its *Partnerships for Peace* policy, which set up a process by which the Eastern European countries will become closer to NATO, leading eventually to full membership.

THE AMERICAN QUESTION

During the Cold War there was no doubt that the close links between the USA and Western Europe were worthwhile and necessary. Now, in the late 1990s, the need for such close cooperation between America and Europe is being questioned on both sides of the Atlantic Ocean.

Some Americans see their military involvement in Europe as being costly and unnecessary. There is no longer any threat from the Soviet Union. Communism is not spreading and the Cold War has been won. There would be some logic in closing down American military bases in Europe and concentrating spending back home in the USA. This would have a major effect on the economies of parts of Germany and England where there are large numbers of American military forces.

Some Europeans would also like to see an end to American military involvement in Europe. They see no need for it now and believe that Europe should develop its own security organisation involving the whole continent.

CONFERENCE ON SECURITY AND COOPERATION IN EUROPE (CSCE)

This includes countries from Western Europe, Eastern Europe and the Commonwealth of Independent States (the former USSR). It is a forum for discussing common security problems and issues.

NATO'S ROLE IN THE FORMER YUGOSLAVIA

Some people believe that NATO's future role should be as a 'world policeman', trying to maintain peace in conflicts around the world.

NATO was brought into the conflict in Bosnia when the United Nations asked for help in policing a 'no-fly zone' around Bosnia.

Serbian aircraft had been bombing Bosnian positions around Sarajevo in total defiance of a 'no-fly zone' which had been agreed before. The UN itself did not have the resources or equipment to police this agreement, so they asked NATO countries to use their air forces to stop the Serbian aircraft (see pages 57–60).

THE WESTERN EUROPEAN UNION (WEU)

The Maastricht Treaty of 1991 brought European countries together in many ways, including moving towards political and monetary union. Maastricht also called on EU members to develop common policies on foreign affairs and security matters.

The Western European Union was formed in 1948 but has been largely inactive over the years because of NATO's role in European security. Now there could be a significant place for the Western European Union as a military and security wing of the European Union. France is especially keen to develop the WEU, saying that Europe should not rely on the USA for defence and security needs, as American troops could be withdrawn from Europe at any time.

Report from the Commons

The scene is the House of Commons in London. The Speaker has just called Mrs Pauline McKenzie, Labour MP for the Scottish constituency of Glenstirling, to ask a question.

Mrs McKenzie – On this side of the House we are very concerned about the fact that UK defence spending is still as high as it was in the past. The Cold War ended years ago. We no longer need the sort of forces which were considered necessary then. Can the Minister explain why our defence spending is still so high?

Minister – Britain has a major role to play within NATO and must honour commitments made to other members. However, we have made cutbacks in the manpower of the armed services, with several regiments being disbanded in the coming year. We feel that this meets our defence needs in the changing world at present.

Mrs McKenzie – But that isn't the real problem, is it? The massive costs for our defence come from our nuclear submarine fleet and the Trident missiles which they carry. To make real savings on defence Britain would need to scrap its nuclear forces.

Minister – Britain has its own nuclear deterrent and that is how it should stay. The government upgraded our Polaris missile system by developing the Trident system as a replacement. Trident is one of the most sophisticated and accurate missile systems in the world. We are the envy of many other nations because we have Trident and they do not.

Mrs McKenzie – We do not need Trident missiles and nuclear submarines in this day and age. Perhaps we should consider the advantages of a strong non-nuclear defence strategy. The threats to peace don't come from major superpowers these days. The former USSR is not a threat, and China is forming strong economic links with the West. The flashpoints nowadays are in places like Yugoslavia. Don't tell me that we would use nuclear missiles there? Britain's future defence role is likely to be as part of international forces keeping the peace in regional conflicts. We should keep our conventional forces as they are, instead of disbanding regiments. Conventional forces are much cheaper to operate and will be of more use in the future than hi-tech nuclear missile systems that could wipe out cities at the press of a button.

Minister – The government believes that we need a balanced defence policy to prepare for all possibilities. Our independent nuclear deterrent makes us safe from attack. There are many countries now with a nuclear capability—what if the likes of Iraq or Libya had nuclear weapons?

Mrs McKenzie – And what about the money that could be saved? That could then be spent on the Health Service, Education and other worthwhile projects. You lot on your side of the House should get your act together and stop making the world a more dangerous place.

Speaker – Order, Order.

PROBLEMS IN THE 1990s FOR NATO

1   There is a great deal of unrest in the former Soviet states.

2   NATO has tried to create a better understanding with the former Communist countries.

TIMETABLE OF CHANGE

1917: Russian Revolution. Communists take power under Lenin.

1924–1953: Stalin rules the USSR and strengthens Communist control over the vast empire.

1985: Gorbachev becomes leader of the USSR, the first of a 'younger generation' of Communists. He promises to change life in the USSR and introduces his new policies of 'glasnost' and 'perestroika'.

1989–1991: The Baltic republics of Latvia, Lithuania and Estonia gain independence from the USSR.

1991: Gorbachev is forced from power by Boris Yeltsin. In December 1991 the USSR and the Communist Party cease to exist.

1992: Establishment of the Commonwealth of Independent States, a loose grouping of newly independent nations which used to be part of the USSR.

1993: A group of hardliners in Parliament refuse to accept economic changes, and in September they occupy the Russian Parliament building. After several days of fighting in Moscow between Parliament forces and Government troops, Boris Yeltsin regains control.

1994: War breaks out in the rebel Chechen Republic. Poverty and unemployment are huge problems across the former Soviet states.

Key to numbered Regions
1   ESTONIA
2   LATVIA
3   LITHUANIA
4   MOLDOVA
5   ARMENIA
6   AZERBAIJAN

Figure 3.2

CRISIS IN THE FORMER SOVIET REPUBLICS

Chechen Republic: In 1991 the Chechens declared their independence from Moscow. This went largely unnoticed until 1994 when Russian troops were sent to Chechenya to bring the rebel republic back into line. Fighting went on for more than a year, with Moscow no closer to imposing control on the Chechens.

Tatarstan: This area refused to join the Russian Federation. In 1994 they signed a Treaty linking them to the Federation, without becoming full members.

Ingush and North Ossetia: These two areas refused to join the Federation. Moscow declared a state of emergency in the areas and sent in troops to take control.

Armenia and Azerbaijan: These two former Soviet

republics have been at war since May 1992 over the disputed region of Nagorny-Karabakh. The Armenians have captured about 10% of Azerbaijan's territory, claiming that it belongs to them as it was allocated to Armenia by Stalin in the 1920s.

Georgia: Civil war has raged since Georgia became independent in 1991. The government has been challenged by rebels led by former President Gamsakhurdia, and by groups demanding independence for the areas of South Ossetia and Abkhazia. Russian peacekeeping forces have been deployed in Georgia.

The Nuclear Threat: The former Soviet Union had a huge store of nuclear weapons. Some of these were dismantled in the late 1980s after agreements with America, but thousands of nuclear warheads remained when the USSR broke up. The whereabouts of all these weapons is unknown, and they could easily fall into the wrong hands. If the leadership of any of the major former Soviet states became hostile to the West, then they would have a ready-made source of nuclear weapons.

Extremists in Russian Politics: It is quite possible that extremist politicians could some day take power in Moscow. The so-called Liberal Democratic Party, led by Vladimir Zhirinovsky, did well in the 1993 elections to the Parliament. Zhirinovsky's policies are nationalist and racist, but he has substantial support amongst ordinary Russians who are fed up with the lack of change under Yeltsin.

The former Communists have also increased in popularity in Russia as people realise that life in the 1970s and '80s was maybe not as bad as they thought. Now they face the problems of unemployment and poverty from which they were sheltered by the Communist regime. In the 1995 parliamentary elections the former Communists were the most successful party, gaining over 20% of the vote.

THE PARTNERSHIP FOR PEACE

The Partnership for Peace Organisation was set up in 1993 for the former Communist countries of Eastern Europe. NATO works closely with the PfP countries, and they are involved in joint training and military exercises. Some PfP countries have adopted NATO equipment.

The aim is to develop a Europe wide commitment to peace and security through greater co-operation and understanding.

Through time it is hoped that PfP countries will join NATO itself.

NATO AND THE WIDER WORLD

NATO is the single most powerful military organisation in the world in the 1990s. Because of this it could be called upon to act to deal with conflicts almost anywhere in the world. During the Gulf War, for example, although the fight against Iraq was carried out under the banner of the United Nations, the forces involved were mainly from NATO countries and the military planning was carried out by NATO generals.

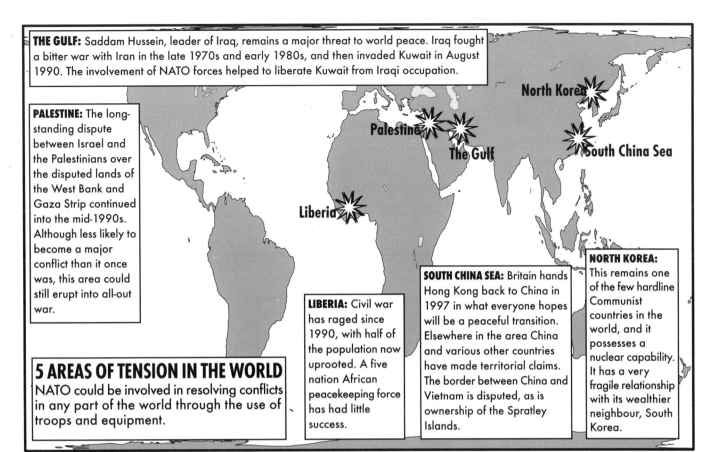

THE GULF: Saddam Hussein, leader of Iraq, remains a major threat to world peace. Iraq fought a bitter war with Iran in the late 1970s and early 1980s, and then invaded Kuwait in August 1990. The involvement of NATO forces helped to liberate Kuwait from Iraqi occupation.

PALESTINE: The long-standing dispute between Israel and the Palestinians over the disputed lands of the West Bank and Gaza Strip continued into the mid-1990s. Although less likely to become a major conflict than it once was, this area could still erupt into all-out war.

5 AREAS OF TENSION IN THE WORLD
NATO could be involved in resolving conflicts in any part of the world through the use of troops and equipment.

LIBERIA: Civil war has raged since 1990, with half of the population now uprooted. A five nation African peacekeeping force has had little success.

SOUTH CHINA SEA: Britain hands Hong Kong back to China in 1997 in what everyone hopes will be a peaceful transition. Elsewhere in the area China and various other countries have made territorial claims. The border between China and Vietnam is disputed, as is ownership of the Spratley Islands.

NORTH KOREA: This remains one of the few hardline Communist countries in the world, and it possesses a nuclear capability. It has a very fragile relationship with its wealthier neighbour, South Korea.

Figure 3.3

Activities

Study Sources 1 and 2, then answer the question which follows.

SOURCE 1

DEVELOPMENT INDICATORS – FORMER SOVIET STATES

	Students in Higher Education (per 10,000 people)	Population Increase per 1,000 per year	Personal Income % with monthly earnings	
			Less Than 75 roubles	Above 200 roubles
Russia	200	6.6	6.3	22.0
Estonia	151	4.3	3.9	33.6
Latvia	164	3.7	3.2	28.3
Lithuania	178	6.1	3.6	24.0
Ukraine	166	3.4	8.1	14.2
Belarus	179	6.2	5.0	19.5
Moldova	126	12.2	13.0	11.0

From *Issues In The New Europe*, Drake, Hodder and Stoughton, 1994

"People throughout the former Soviet Union have benefited from the changes of the 1990s."
(View of a Moscow journalist.)

SOURCE 2
The people of most of the former Soviet States have enjoyed improved democracy in the 1990s. Elections have taken place in most of the Republics, but not in Tajikistan where opposition parties are still banned and the Communist Party still has power. Living standards in most parts of the former USSR have improved for some people who can afford to buy the better range of goods now available in the shops. However, for some people who have lost their jobs, poverty is now a reality with beggars on the streets of many cities.

The republics closest to Europe—Belarus, Ukraine and the Baltic States—have the best chance of improving their economies, while those in Central Asia such as Tajikistan, Azerbaijan and Kazakhstan are likely to remain very poor for a long time to come.

Using the information in Sources 1 and 2 above, provide evidence for and against the view of the journalist. Overall do you think the evidence supports the view?

CHAPTER 3

MILITARY ALLIANCES IN EUROPE – SECTION 3
THE ARMS RACE AND DISARMAMENT

What you will learn

1   The development of nuclear weapons and the theory of deterrence.

2   Progress in Arms Reduction Treaties.

THE ARMS RACE

From the early 1950s through to the late 1980s the USA and the USSR were engaged in an 'Arms Race'. Both sides tried to develop more and more nuclear weapons, and to make them ever more powerful and accurate.

DETERRENCE

Both sides argued that having all these weapons made the world a safer place. The two superpowers disagreed with each other on many issues of ideology, but each was frightened to start a war with the other. They knew that whoever started the war could not win, because their opponents were so heavily armed. The outcome of nuclear war would have been destruction for both sides. Because they knew what the consequences would be, this became known as the *Theory of Deterrence*.

THE NUCLEAR AGE

The race to produce nuclear weapons began during World War Two. It was known that it would be possible to develop weapons with vast destructive power and both the Americans and the Germans started programmes to produce 'the bomb'.

Time ran out for the German scientists with the defeat of their armies in May 1945, just at the time when the Americans had made the breakthrough. They continued the development work and in August 1945 two Atomic bombs were dropped on the Japanese cities of Hiroshima and Nagasaki.

The destruction was enormous. Seventy thousand people died within seconds in Hiroshima, and over 250,000 died there in total. The figures were repeated at Nagasaki.

The bombs used on Japan in 1945 were tiny compared to the devices developed in the 1970s and '80s. These could have a destructive force 5,000 times as great as the Hiroshima bomb.

The attack on Japan was carried out by dropping the bombs from aircraft. Nowadays it is possible to deliver the nuclear warhead to its target in many different ways: by land-based cruise missile, by submarine-launched missile, by shell, by bomb or by intercontinental rocket.

The prospect of nuclear war frightened the world from the 1960s until the late 1980s. The superpowers possessed the weapons to wipe out the earth's population many times over.

Today there are still thousands of nuclear weapons in existence, but the chances of them being used have lessened. Leaders of both the USA and the USSR tried, at various times, to make agreements to reduce the number of nuclear and conventional weapons held by each side. The details are given in the *Factfile* on page 53.

FACTFILE: Arms Agreements

1963 Partial Test Ban Treaty
The USA, the USSR and the UK agreed to stop testing nuclear weapons in the atmosphere. France continued to do so.

1968 Nuclear Non-Proliferation Treaty
This treaty was designed to stop the spread of the knowledge and the technology required to make nuclear weapons. In theory each country with nuclear weapons must have developed them by themselves, with their own expertise and raw materials.

1972 Strategic Arms Limitation Treaty (SALT 1)
This treaty set upper limits for how many long-range nuclear missiles each country could have.

1979 SALT 2
Extended the previous talks and set new limits for strategic nuclear missiles.

1987 INF Treaty (Intermediate Nuclear Forces)
This treaty dealt with short- and medium-range nuclear missiles—the type which could be used in Europe. All land based weapons in these categories were to be destroyed within three years, and the USA and USSR had access to each other's sites for verification of the Treaty.

The INF Treaty did not include submarine launched missiles.

1990 Convential Forces in Europe Treaty (CFE)

The Warsaw Pact countries always had a huge advantage in numbers of conventional weapons. This treaty evened out the military balance in Europe, setting maximum numbers for tanks, artillery, armoured vehicles etc.

1991 Strategic Arms Reduction Treaty (START 1)
Around 30% of the really destructive Intercontinental Ballistic Missiles were destroyed. These are the type of missiles which could be launched from the USA and wipe out Moscow within an hour. There will be a maximum of 6,000 nuclear warheads by the year 2000, each still capable of killing hundreds of thousands of people.

1993 START 2
This Treaty built on progress made in START 1. All Intercontinental Ballistic Missiles are to be eliminated from the year 2003. Only Submarine Launched and mobile warheads will remain. The total number of nuclear warheads will be reduced from 6,000 to about 3,500.

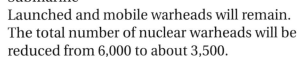

1 **"The destructive power of nuclear weapons is enormous."**

Give evidence to support this statement.

2 How do modern nuclear weapons differ from those dropped on Japan in 1945?

3 What is meant by 'the Arms Race'?

4 What is meant by 'Deterrence'?

5 What major breakthrough in limiting nuclear weapons was achieved in 1987?

6 How many nuclear warheads will be allowed under the START 2 Treaty?

Now read the information in Source 1 below and answer the question which follows.

7 **"START 1 and START 2 do not really make Europe any safer. In fact, it can be argued that they have made Europe a more dangerous place."**

Give evidence to support and oppose this view.

Overall do you think the evidence supports the view?

A MORE DANGEROUS EUROPE?

Treaties such as START 1 and START 2 seem to make the world a much safer place by reducing the number of nuclear weapons. But do they? Could they actually make Europe a more dangerous place in the future?

WHEN the two superpowers had stocks of huge Intercontinental Missiles targeted on each other's main cities, then the chances of them ever being used were very slight. If the Soviet Union had launched an attack firing missiles at New York and Washington, then the Americans could have detected them coming. They would have fired missiles back at places such as Moscow and Leningrad. Surely neither side would have been stupid enough to have started a conflict in this way.

START 2 eliminates these missiles which could wipe out a city and make it uninhabitable for decades. Instead, the main powers will be left with smaller nuclear weapons with a more limited range. It is possible that a country might be tempted to use these, knowing that it would not bring about global destruction. However, in the area where they were used there would be massive destruction and loss of life. The most likely place to use them could be in Europe.

Of course the superpowers have had these smaller weapons for many years, so why did they not use them before now, at the height of the Cold War? The answer is simple—any war which started with small nuclear devices would quickly escalate to bring in the huge Intercontinental Missiles. Now that they are no longer present, does the theory of deterrence still work?

The changes in the former Soviet Union and Eastern Europe have made a massive difference to world affairs. If you had suggested in 1980 that by 1990 the Berlin Wall would be down, the Soviet Union disbanded and democratic elections under way in Russia then people would have thought that you were mad.

Things could change just as quickly in the future. Extremist groups are growing in popularity in the former Soviet Union. The war in the former Yugoslavia could escalate. Saddam Hussein could develop and use his own nuclear weapons. We cannot be sure that the world, and Europe in particular, are safer places than they were before.

Source 1

1 Methods used by the UNO to try and maintain peace and security.

2 The causes, nature and possible outcomes of the war in the former Yugoslavia.

3 Methods used by the UNO to try and maintain peace in the area.

FACTFILE: UN Organisation

THE ORGANISATION OF THE UNITED NATIONS

The International Court of Justice

The International Court of Justice, based in The Hague, deals with human rights issues.

The General Assembly

The General Assembly of the United Nations is the main forum for debate and discussion. All of the members—there were 184 in 1995—have a seat in the General Assembly and they have one vote each, no matter how large or small they are. The General Assembly decides on many issues to do with the United Nations, but peacekeeping and conflict are the responsibility of the Security Council.

The Security Council

The Security Council consists of 15 members. Five of these are permanent members (China, France, Russia, the UK and the USA), and ten are nonpermanent members. These change every two years, with five of them coming from Africa and Asia, one from Eastern Europe, two from Latin America and two from Western Europe and the rest of the world. Some members of the UN want the number of permanent members to be reduced.

Economic and Social Council

The Economic and Social Council coordinates the work of the many UN Specialised Agencies. These carry out the economic and social role of the United Nations, trying to improve living standards in poorer parts of the world. The work of the Specialised Agencies is dealt with on pages 20–24.

The Secretariat

The UN Secretariat is like a civil service for all the other parts of the United Nations. It is headed by the *Secretary General* of the UN, currently Boutros Boutros-Ghali of Egypt. The job of Secretary General is a very important one as he is present at all important UN events and can act as a personal mediator in disputes between states.

PEACEKEEPING AND THE UN

The effectiveness of the UN has grown since the end of the Cold War. The United States and the Soviet Union used to block each other's attempts to find peace in international disputes, but now the UN is free from that type of political action.

When the Iraqis invaded Kuwait in 1990, the UN took collective security action to remove them. The American and British forces who fought in the Gulf did so under the banner of the United Nations and they were there as representatives of the whole UN organisation.

Peacekeeping Force – Forces drawn from UN members patrol a troubled area to try and keep the warring sides apart. These UN Forces are known as the 'Blue Berets' because of their distinctive uniform. Such a force has been used in the former Yugoslavia.

Since the UN was established, the Security Council has organised many peacekeeping forces around the world. Some of the current forces include:

UNFICYP – UN peacekeeping force in Cyprus

UNPROFOR – UN protection force in the former Yugoslavia. (Withdrawn December 1995.)

UNOMIG – UN observer mission in Georgia.

UN ACTION

The UN tries to prevent the outbreak of war by making countries cooperate with each other. If war does break out, then the UN tries to bring it to an end as quickly as possible. The UN is also trying to limit the spread of weapons and reduce the numbers of particularly dangerous chemical and nuclear weapons in the world.

The UN Security Council has a number of options when dealing with a conflict.

Fact Finding Missions – The UN can send a delegation to investigate a conflict and they will then report back to the General Assembly and the Security Council.

Military Observers – UN officials patrol a ceasefire arrangement between countries which are engaged in a conflict.

Economic Sanctions – The UN can ask member states to stop trading with a country if they want to put that nation under pressure. Economic sanctions were imposed on Serbia to try and change its policy in Bosnia.

Arms Sanctions – The UN can ask member states to stop dealing in arms and munitions with a particular country. This can be used to cut off supplies which are being used in a war.

PROBLEMS WITH UN PEACEKEEPING

Increase in Peacekeeping Duties: There has been a big increase in the number of UN peacekeeping forces in recent years.

1991 – Iraq / Kuwait, Angola, El Salvador, Western Sahara

1992 – Croatia, Bosnia, Macedonia, Mozambique

1993 – Somalia, Uganda, Rwanda, Georgia, Liberia, Haiti

Escalating Cost
Supporting all the peacekeeping forces has become very expensive. The UN is in real danger of running out of money. Major countries like the USA and the UK do not like having to keep increasing their contributions.

Casualties
Countries which have sent troops to form part of peacekeeping forces are concerned at rising numbers of casualties.

Lack of Success in Peacekeeping Efforts
Both in the former Yugoslavia and in Somalia the UN forces have been criticised for failing to keep the peace effectively. They argue that their hands are tied and that they cannot act effectively. The whole concept of UN peacekeeping forces is being called into question.

1   How powerful is the General Assembly of the United Nations?

2   Who are the five permanent members of the Security Council?

3   What work is organised by the Economic and Social Council?

4   **"The UN has become more effective since the end of the Cold War."**

    Give evidence to support this statement.

5   How does the UN try to prevent war and conflict?

6   What options does the UN have when conflict does start?

7   Who are 'the Blue Berets'?

8   List three places in Europe where UN Peacekeeping Forces were based in 1995.

9   Imagine you are an accountant working in the UN Secretariat Financial Section. Write a short report for the Secretary General in which you highlight the problems of recent peacekeeping missions.

    Your report should be about 120 words in length.

10 The UN Secretary General replies saying that it is vital that peacekeeping missions continue. Do you agree with this view? Give reasons for your answer.

THE UNITED NATIONS IN YUGOSLAVIA

Countdown to Disaster – the break-up of Yugoslavia

1988 – The province of Kosovo, where the population is split between Serbs and Albanians, witnesses rioting and disturbances. Serbs claim they have been victimised by Albanians.

1989 – Serb President Slobodan Milosevic takes over the semi-independent provinces of Kosovo and Vojvodina. This is seen as part of the establishment of a 'Greater Serbia'.

1990 – Croatia and Slovenia threaten to leave Yugoslavia unless Serbia stops expanding.

1991 – Croatia and Slovenia declare independence. Serbia sends in its army to try and bring them back into line. Serbia takes over substantial areas of Croatia.

1992 – UNPROFOR sends 14,000

The Republics of the former Yugoslavia

Figure 3.4

troops to Croatia. Serbs living in Croatia demand to be included in 'Greater Serbia'.

War breaks out in Bosnia. Bosnian

Muslims and Croats vote to declare independence, but Bosnian Serbs, backed by the regular Serbian army, become involved in an armed conflict.

57

BACKGROUND TO THE CONFLICT

Yugoslavia was formed at the end of World War One as a Confederation of different republics in the Western Balkans area. The country always experienced unrest and mistrust between the different nationalities, who did not even share the same language, religion or culture. However, from the 1940s until the early 1980s this caused few problems. Yugoslavia had a very strong leader, President Tito, who kept a firm control over the country. His Socialist government was not always popular, but he did make Yugoslavia the most prosperous of the Eastern European countries. Although a Communist himself, Tito kept his independence from Moscow.

It was only when Tito died that the different groups within Yugoslavia became more noticeable and the country moved quickly to break-up and civil war.

THE WAR IN BOSNIA

Bosnia is a small, landlocked country, with Serbia to the east and Croatia to the west. Bosnia's capital is Sarajevo. The population is about 4.1 million, of whom 43% are Bosnian Muslims, 32% are Serbs and 17% are Croats.

Each ethnic group has its own areas where they dominate the population. Other areas have a mixed population. The Muslims and Croats voted for in-

dependence early in 1992, but the Bosnian Serbs were against the move. They wanted to be integrated with 'Greater Serbia', and so the war began.

The war in Bosnia was particularly nasty, with atrocities committed by all sides. A policy of 'ethnic cleansing' was used by the Bosnian Serbs to drive Muslims out of the Serb held areas. Villages were torched and people were murdered as the situation got out of hand.

THE ROLE OF THE UNITED NATIONS

From October 1992 United Nations forces were sent to Bosnia to protect aid convoys. Vital supplies of food and medicines were being stopped by the Serbs who had tightened their grip around Sarajevo. UN troops were given orders to protect the convoys, but not to become involved in the fighting.

The European Union and the United Nations set up a joint negotiating team to try and bring the different groups around the conference table. They put forward a peace plan, known as the Vance-Owen Plan, which proposed dividing Bosnia into ten semi-independent provinces—three each for the Serbs, the Croats and the Bosnian Muslims, and one mixed province.

The Croats and Muslims accepted the plan, and after much delay so did the leader of the Bosnia Serbs, Radovan Karadzic. However, his Parliament rejected the proposal and the Vance-Owen Plan failed.

The UN imposed total trade and diplomatic sanctions on Serbia in protest at its military involvement in Bosnia.

Early in 1993 the UN declared the towns of Sarajevo, Srebrenica, Bihac and Gorazde as 'Safe Areas'. They had previously been under attack from Serb artillery and air forces.

However, the Serbs continued their attacks on Sarajevo and seemed poised to capture the city until NATO issued an ultimatum for them to withdraw or face air attacks.

The Serbs pulled back, but continued an artillery bombardment of Sarajevo. When 60 civilians were killed by a shell in a Sarajevo marketplace, NATO again issued an ultimatum for the Serbs to remove their heavy artillery from the area or hand it over to the United Nations forces. Again, in the face of NATO pressure, the Serbs gave in. Russia sent troops to Sarajevo to put further pressure on the Serbs, its former allies.

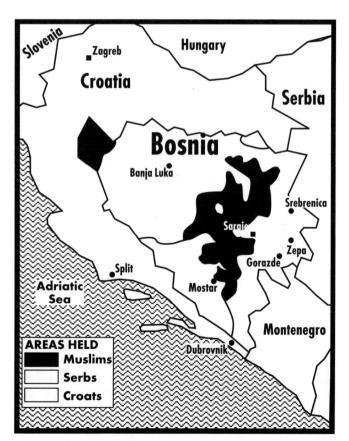

Figure 3.5   Bosnia in 1994

Civilian protesters often made it difficult for the UN to carry out its role

OBSERVATIONS ABOUT THE PEACEKEEPING EFFORTS

- The UN forces found their job to be virtually impossible. Their aim was to protect aid convoys and they were powerless to intervene, even when witnessing atrocities. Several UN commanders expressed disgust because they knew who was responsible, but could do nothing about it.

- Countries like Britain and France became more reluctant to commit troops to the UN forces.

- Serbia blatantly ignored the UN Security Council's No Fly Zone over Bosnia, and also the UN Safe Areas set up in Bosnia. The UN asked NATO to enforce the No Fly Zones.

- NATO was much more effective at putting pressure on the warring groups, especially the Serbs. NATO action, or the threat of NATO action, often had the desired effect.

- The NATO action was at the request of the European members. American involvement was less than it would have been in the past.

- UN sanctions on Serbia were effective and they were enforced with the help of the Western European Union (WEU). The sanctions were lifted late in 1994.

- In 1995 the International Court of Justice began the first War Crimes Trials to be held since the end of World War Two.

- Both NATO and the WEU said that they would commit forces to an International Peacekeeping Force following the signing of a peace agreement.

- Humanitarian aid reached civilians due to the work of the UN forces.

THE REFUGEE PROBLEM

One consequence of the war in Yugoslavia was the creation of many thousands of refugees. Some people moved to other parts of the former Yugoslavia while others fled the country entirely and moved to Germany, Austria and other countries.

In 1995 the United Nations High Commission for Refugees (UNHCR) calculated that about 3 million people had been displaced since 1992. They have the job of trying to deal with the refugees and ensuring that they can live in decent conditions. This task was made more difficult because the Safe Havens established by the United Nations came under repeated attack from Serb forces.

59

PEACE IN BOSNIA?

In December 1995, a peace agreement came into effect in Bosnia. Representatives of all the warring factions had met at a United States Air Force Base at Dayton, Ohio, where they negotiated a deal to end the conflict.

1995 had witnessed the decline of Bosnian Serb dominance. Croatia had recaptured Western Slovenia and Karjina and NATO's air power was finally unleashed on the Bosnian Serbs. It was clear that the lightly armed UN troops, operating under highly restricted rules, had failed to maintain the peace. The turning point came in September 1995 when, after a Sarjevo mortar attack by the Bosnian Serbs, NATO launched intensive aerial bombardments on their army. The Serb leader, Slobodan Milosevic, eager for an end to economic sanctions, supported the American envoy, Richard Holbrooke, in his search for peace. The Bosnian Serbs were now vulnerable and isolated and had no choice but to give Milosevic authority to negotiate for them.

Under the December 1995 agreement Bosnia remains a single state with one capital but two entities. A federation of its Croats and Muslims has 51% of the land, including Sarajevo, while its Serbs in the north and east have the remaining 49% of the land. Both areas have a separate parliament and president but there is also a central government based in Sarajevo.

In order to supervise the establishment of the new country, NATO sent a force of 60,000 troops to Bosnia. They took over from the UNPROFOR peacekeepers who had been powerless to prevent conflict in Bosnia. The NATO force, known as IFOR, went with a different set of instructions. Their role was to enforce the Dayton Agreement. The United States provided the bulk of the troops for IFOR, but other countries, including Britain and Russia, were involved. It is the first time that NATO forces have been deployed in this way since the formation of the organisation in 1949.

Figure 3.6

Map legend:
- Proposed new boundary
- Land under Serbian control
- Land under Bosnian and Croatian control

THE NATO PEACEKEEPING FORCE (IFOR)

➤ 60,000 NATO troops including a 2,500-strong Rapid Reaction Force in Sarajevo

➤ 20,000 United States troops, based in Tuzla, armed with tanks, armoured vehicles and helicopters.

➤ 13,000 British soldiers based in Gornji Vakuf.

➤ 13,500 French, Spanish and Italian troops in Sarajevo.

➤ 4,000 German medical and logistic troops based at Split in Croatia.

➤ 2,000 Russian troops at the Posavina corridor in northern Bosnia. Although not NATO members, the Russian troops will take their orders from the NATO forces.

THE PRICE OF PEACE

✝ It is not clear how many people died in the Bosnian war. The Muslim led government of Bosnia suggested that as many as 150,000 of its citizens were killed, but international observers think that this figure was exaggerated.

✝ 200 UN soldiers died in Bosnia.

WAR CRIMES IN THE FORMER YUGOSLAVIA

After the fragile peace was established in Bosnia in late 1995, evidence grew of war crimes and atrocities committed during the bloody civil war. The IFOR supervised peace allowed journalists and investigators to visit areas which had been impossible to see during the hostilities.

As long ago as 1992, the American State Department had said that atrocities in Bosnia were the worst seen in Europe since the days of the Nazis. At that time it had become clear that the Serbs had a number of prisons in the Prijedor area which were run like concentration camps.

The UN convened an International War Crimes Tribunal in 1994 and 52 people were indicted. This means that they were effectively charged with committing war crimes. Those indicted included Radovan Karadzic and Ratko Mladic, the two Bosnian Serb leaders, both accused of genocide and crimes against humanity. By February 1996, the UN High Commissioner for Refugees had found evidence of 187 mass graves in the former Yugoslavia, 13 of which were said to contain at least 500 bodies. However, only one of the fifty two indicted people was in custody—Dusan Tadicm was charged with murdering and raping Muslims and Croats during the brutal process of ethnic cleansing around Prijedor in 1992.

Activities

1 **"The death of Tito was the event which plunged Yugoslavia into chaos."**

Give evidence to support this statement.

2 What happened in Croatia and Slovenia in 1991?

3 Which part of the former Yugoslavia seemed to be trying to expand into other areas?

4 **"Bosnia has a mixed population."**

Give evidence to support this statement.

5 What is meant by 'ethnic cleansing'?

6 What role did the UN take on from October 1992?

7 Why did the UN set up Safe Areas in 1993?

8 Study the information in the section *Observations About the Peacekeeping Efforts.*

"NATO has been more effective than the United Nations in helping the situation in Bosnia."

(View of a former British Army officer who served in Bosnia.)

Provide evidence for and against the view of the former British Army officer. Overall do you agree with the view?

9 What is the job of UNHCR?

What you will learn

1   The USA is a powerful country.

2   The US population is made up of different ethnic groups.

USA

Area: 9,809,390 square kilometres

Capital: Washington, DC (1990 population 606,900)

Largest city: New York (1990 population 7,322,564)

Population: 254,521,000

Distribution: 74% urban, 26% rural

New York
Washington DC

The United States is the fourth largest country in the world after the Russian Federation, Canada, and China. It is 9,809,390 square kilometres in area. (The UK is only 244,100 square kilometres.) With a population of 260 million (including illegal immigrants) in 1992, the USA has the third largest population in the world (after China and India). The USA also has a large variety of mineral, agricultural, water and other land resources which provide the basis for a highly productive economy making the United States the world's wealthiest nation.

The United States is a leading country in world affairs and is an influential member of such international organisations as the United Nations (headquarters in New York City) and the World Bank (headquarters in Washington, DC). It was also a leader in a number of defence organisations such as the North Atlantic Defence Organisation. The USA has a large number of nuclear weapons and had, perhaps, the most powerful conventional forces in the world.

CLIMATE

The United States is so large that much of the interior of the country has a continental climate with extremes of temperature and rainfall. Around the coasts the oceans moderate the extremes of temperature.

Some parts of the USA get more than 2,500mm of rainfall each year, whereas other areas get less than 250mm. The country's temperatures are as varied. In New York the average annual temperature is 13°C (55°F). Farther south around Charleston, South Carolina, a subtropical zone, the average annual temperature is 19°C (66°F). Farther south still in Miami, a tropical zone, the average temperature is 24°C (75°F).

THE ECONOMY

By 1992 the gross national product (GNP) of the United States was $5.9 trillion, the highest in the world. (Compare this with a GNP of $915.5 billion in the UK.) The percapita income of almost $23,000 is also among the world's highest (UK $15,600).

Agriculture, fishing and forestry together contribute about 2% to the GNP. Cut timber earns about $1 billion annually and income from the US fishing industry was $3.5 billion in 1988.

Manufacturing contributes about 20% to the GNP. The United States is a world leader in the production and export of various types of machinery, including office and telecommunication equipment and transportation equipment such as automobiles. It is also a major producer and exporter of industrial raw materials and chemicals.

Mining accounts for only about 2% of the GNP but produced $123.8 billion in 1987, nearly 80% of which was derived from mineral fuels—coal, natural gas, and petroleum.

WE THE AMERICAN PEOPLE

DIFFERENT ETHNIC GROUPS IN THE USA (1990)

	Number (million)	%
White	200	77
Black (African Americans)	30	11
Native American	2	1
Asian and Pacific Islanders	7	3
Hispanic	21	8

Table 4.1

WHITE AMERICANS

This is the largest single group in the US in the 1990s. There are 200 million white Americans who have largely been assimilated into the American culture by the education system. If we look more closely around the US, however, we see that there are cultural differences between white Americans. While the education system tries to create American citizens, attitudes to life are shaped by both the envi-

Irish-Americans retain strong links with 'the old country'. The largest St Patrick's Day parade in the world is held in New York City.

ronment in which people find themselves and the culture they are handed down from their ancestors.

Up to 1860, most migrants to the US were from northern Europe. These people settled in all areas of the USA. Between 1860 and 1920 white migrants came mainly from eastern and southern Europe. They remained mainly in the eastern states and worked in the cities.

After one or two generations in the US many of these people began to mix and so gave rise to the idea of the melting pot in US society (see page 65). Nevertheless, to this day there are many areas of the USA which still retain differences brought about by the cultures, customs and religions of the original groups which settled in that particular area.

THE NATIVE AMERICAN

Native Americans are the descendants of the original migrants to America who arrived between 20,000 and 40,000 years ago across the land bridge which once connected Alaska with Kamchatka in Asia. Today there are about 2 million Native Americans in the USA. Most are descended

The Native American is one of the poorest groups in the USA.

from the Indian tribes which were destroyed by the advance of the white settlers. The group also includes the Eskimo and Aleuts who live in Alaska.

Most Native Americans live west of the Mississippi River in the States of Oklahoma, New Mexico, Arizona, South Dakota and California. About 50% live on or near the 287 reservations identified by the Federal Government. These cover about 54 million acres of land. Native Americans have improved their lives in the past 20 years by working through pressure groups to get the government to make concessions and provide financial settlements for past misdeeds. However, life for many on the reservations is still difficult. 50% of young Native Americans on reservations do not graduate from high school. Unemployment rates are 40% or higher and birth and death rates are higher than the US average. Also, the suicide rate is twice the rate for the US.

AFRICAN AMERICANS

The 30 million African Americans or black Americans trace their ancestors back to the slaves brought over to the USA from Africa to work on the plantations of the southern States in the 17th and 18th

CELEBRATE AFRICAN-AMERICAN HERITAGE

American schools highlight African American history every year.

centuries. Slightly more than half of this group are concentrated in the states of the south and southeast and the rest are to be found in the industrial cities of the northeast, central and Pacific coast states.

African Americans have been very influential in the political, economic and social life of the USA —both directly and indirectly. The Civil War (1860–1865) was fought over the extension of and then the existence of slavery. Politics in the 1950s and 1960s was dominated by the civil rights movement. Politics in the 1980s and 1990s was heavily influenced by the turnout of the African American vote.

HISPANIC AMERICANS

These are people living in the US who belong to Spanish-speaking ethnic groups. There are 21 million Hispanics in the US. This group is made up of Mexican Americans, Puerto Ricans, Cubans and those from Central and South America.

Mexican Americans The border with Mexico is over 1,000 miles long and many Mexicans have come to settle in the states of the southwest and the Pacific coast. They leave Mexico because of poverty and unemployment. They are one of the most economically deprived groups in the US with 25% living below the poverty line. They often work in low-paid jobs in the towns or as low-paid farm labour.

Puerto Ricans are citizens of the US by birth. They travel freely between Puerto Rico and the US. They are concentrated mainly in New York and other east coast cities. As a group they have the lowest income level in the nation and have the highest unemployment rates for Hispanics. They come to the US because of the population pressure, unemployment and poverty in Puerto Rico.

Cubans are mainly concentrated in Florida and to some extent in New York and New Jersey. Some originally fled the revolution in Cuba in 1959 and since then, because of the economic hardships in Cuba, many have crossed the 90 miles to the USA. Many are middle-class people and businessmen who have improved the economy of Florida. A significant number were involved in criminal activities in Cuba and have since made Miami one of the

centres for smuggling drugs, especially cocaine, into the USA. This has increased the crime and murder rate in Florida enormously.

Central and South America There are a number of immigrants to the USA from countries such as Nicaragua, El Salvador, Colombia, Chile etc. These people have fled from the poverty and political persecution they face in their country of origin.

ASIAN AND PACIFIC ISLANDERS

Over 7 million Americans came to the US from Asia or the Pacific Islands. They are from three areas:

1 East Asia – Chinese, Japanese and Koreans

2 Southeast Asia – Cambodians, Laotians, Thai and Vietnamese

3 The Pacific Islands – Fijians, Filipinos, Guamanians, Hawaiians and Samoans.

Many Chinese Americans arrived in the US during the gold rush of the 1850s. They soon became involved largely in the service sector, being barred from many occupations by law. Many Chinese people congregated in Chinatowns in the main cities. More Chinese people arrived, mainly from Hong Kong, after 1965.

Japanese Americans arrived in significant numbers after the 1880s to provide cheap labour. They later moved into trades and small businesses, but their success angered many Americans and they suffered from discrimination.

Korean American immigration has mainly been from the 1960s to the 1990s. This is a highly educated group. Over half of this group are dispersed throughout cities of the north-east and mid-west. The rest are working on the west coast.

The number of Filipino Americans rapidly increased between 1960 and 1990 and there are now 1.5 million in the US. Until the 1960s, Filipinos were discriminated against and prevented from getting good jobs. Today, many are professionals and their children attain high levels of education. As a result, the standard of living of this group has improved.

A number of Pacific Islanders have had difficulty adjusting to life in the US and the education system has not been very sympathetic to their needs. There are 211,000 Hawaiians, 63,000 Samoans and 50,000 Guamanians living throughout the US.

Cambodians, Laotians and Vietnamese came to the US after 1975 when the Vietnam War ended. There are about 1 million Americans in this ethnic group, and while many are highly educated, most have had

Many Asian Americans are very successful in education and business.

to settle for low-paid jobs in the US. Many are taking the traditional way out by starting up their own businesses, especially in the service sector.

SO WHAT IS AN AMERICAN?

There are different theories about what happens to immigrants once they settle in the USA.

One of these theories is the *melting pot*. Think about making a cup of coffee. You need hot water, coffee, sugar and milk. You mix them all together and you get a cup of brown liquid. You cannot pick out the spoonful of coffee or the spoonful of sugar. This is the melting pot theory. No matter how the people in the USA start out—Vietnamese, Cuban, African American—once they have been in the USA for a while they become 'American' and lose their individual identity.

Another theory is the *salad bowl*. Think about making a salad. You get lettuce, tomato, cucumber, onion and pepper and mix them together in a bowl. However, this time you can still pick out the different ingredients. The idea here is that the different ethnic groups mix together to create an American society, but retain their own identities and cultures to enrich that society.

A new theory is that of the *mosaic*. A mosaic is a pattern of different colours. Some pieces are just one colour and some are a mixture of colours. The idea is that people in the USA would have a choice about what they wanted to be—either an 'American' or else keep their own identity and culture.

Activities

1 **'The USA is a powerful country.'**
Select appropriate information and either
a) write a report using this title or
b) make up a leaflet entitled *The USA is a powerful country.*
Consider the following: size, population, wealth, military power.

2 Here is a list of US businesses:

Boeing	Levi Strauss	Pepsicola
Coca-Cola	IBM	Apple
Motorola	HJ Heinz	Gillette
General Motors	Ford Motors	Exxon
Mobil	TEXACO	Avon
Safeway	Procter and Gamble	Xerox
Kodak	Johnson & Johnson	Goodyear
Colgate-Palmolive	Unilever	

Make up a table showing the name of the company, what it produces and the number of people in the class who have used its products.

This will require you to survey the class. Write up your results.

3 Study Table 4.1 showing ethnic groups in the USA in 1990. Use the information in the table to construct a pie chart. Give it an appropriate title and explain what it shows.

4 In this activity you will practise the skill of note taking. The first one has been done for you.

   White Americans
   ● largest group
   ● 200 million people
   ● migrated from Europe
   ● settled in all parts of the USA
   ● mixed well in US society after one or two generations

a) Copy the bullet points on White Americans.

b) For the following ethnic groups, make up your own notes (bullet points):

   Hispanic Americans   African Americans
   Native Americans   Asian and Pacific Islanders

5 Read the information on *So what is an American?* Make your own notes under the following headings:

   Melting Pot;   Salad Bowl;   Mosaic.

CHAPTER 4

THE USA – SECTION 2

THE AMERICAN DREAM

What you will learn

1 Why people move to the USA.

2 What the American Dream is.

3 Why American people want to limit immigration in the 1990s.

Many Americans believe they are born equal. They believe that the USA is a democratic country and that any American citizen can be elected President. They think that they are free to live their lives the way they want to and that the USA is full of wealth and opportunities. Anyone can be successful and wealthy if they work hard. This is the dream, but not the reality for many.

> *"...the land of the free*
> *And the home of the brave."*

Each verse of the US National Anthem ends with these words. It is what many Americans think. It is part of the American Dream. The American Dream is about equality and freedom. It is about individuals having rights and opportunities. These themes run through the Declaration of Independence and the Constitution of the United States.

The Declaration of Independence states "…that all men are created equal…" and that governments exist to guarantee "life, liberty and the pursuit of happiness". If a government fails to do that, then it is "the right of the people to alter or abolish it, and to institute a new government." Therefore the arguments used to justify the creation of the United States are the basis of the American Dream. All people are equal. People have the right to freedom and the opportunity to find happiness.

Throughout the twentieth century, popular culture through film and then TV projected an image of the US to the world. That image constantly portrayed the US as a wealthy country, a land of opportunity where people could improve their living standards with hard work, where people enjoyed freedoms and basic human rights.

Therefore the American Dream is about equality, freedom, rights and opportunities in the political, social and economic areas of people's lives.

DEMOCRACY AND THE AMERICAN DREAM

The US is a democratic republic. This describes the political nature of the country. Republican government is where power rests with the people and their elected representatives. The head of state is elected. This is unlike a monarchy which has a ruler who inherits the post and is the source of all power in the country.

A democracy is where people elect representatives to make decisions for them and may replace these representatives at a future election if they do not like the decisions they have taken. US citizens are able to vote for the people they want. They can stand as candidates in an election. Many people want to live in the USA because it is a very democratic country.

We can see on the Ballot Paper on page 67 that the voter has to choose 8 people for 8 different jobs. As well as this, the voter will be able to vote for a President, a Vice-President, a Senator and a member of the House of Representatives—another four jobs.

Americans can also take part in a state referendum. A referendum is when the people can vote for or against an issue. The outcome of the referendum is binding on the government of the state. Referenda are examples of direct democracy. Here are some examples of questions which might be asked in a referendum.

- ✗ Do you think California should keep the death penalty?
- ✗ Should Kentucky should cut income tax by 10 cents?
- ✗ Should New York ban cars from the centre of the city to stop air pollution?

USA	Ballot Paper
FOR STATE SENATOR District 33 (Vote for one)	☐
Joe Clay Hamilton (Democrat Party)	
FOR STATE REPRESENTATIVE District 83 (Vote for one)	☐
Norma Bourdeaux (Democrat Party)	
Gene Bryan (Republican Party)	☐
FOR GOVERNOR (Vote for one)	☐
Kirk Fordice (Republican Party)	
Ray Mabus (Democrat Party)	☐
Shawn O'Hara (Independent)	
THE LIEUTENANT GOVERNOR (Vote for one)	☐
Eddie Briggs (Republican Party)	
Brad Dye (Democrat Party)	☐
Henry Kirksey (Independent)	
FOR SHERIFF (Vote for one)	☐
PG Gunnis Hill (Democrat Party)	
Everett W Keller (Republican Party)	☐
FOR TAX COLLECTOR (Vote for one)	☐
Charles E Tingle (Democrat Party)	
FOR JUSTICE COURT JUDGE District Three (Vote for one)	☐
William 'Bill' Gunn (Democrat Party)	
Johnny Stokes Riddle (Independent)	☐
Randy Rose (Republican Party)	☐
FOR CITY DOG CATCHER (Vote for one)	☐
Aaron London (Republican Party)	
Pearson M Milhous (Democrat Party)	☐

CAPITALISM AND THE AMERICAN DREAM

The US is a capitalist country. Capitalism is an ideology which describes the way a country organises its economic activity. In a capitalist country individuals are free to invest in any business they choose. If they are successful, they will make profits and become wealthy, but if they make losses their businesses will close. Competition and demand decide whether a business will be successful or not. Competition from other companies will force a firm to cut its prices and provide better services to attract customers. The successful businesses will drive out the less competitive ones. Businesses will only be successful if they provide what the public demand ie. are willing to pay for.

Under capitalism, people can set up their own companies. They can invest their money, talents, abilities and their hard work and if they are successful they will achieve the American Dream. Figure 4.1 gives some evidence that Americans have benefited from capitalism.

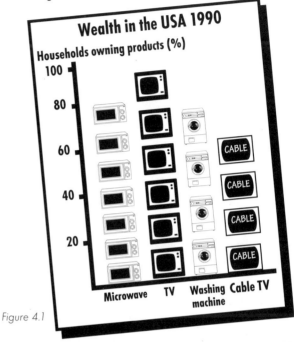

Figure 4.1

RIGHTS AND FREEDOMS AND THE AMERICAN DREAM

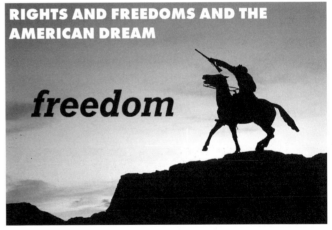

The rights of people in the USA are an important aspect of the American Dream. The rights of all Americans are enshrined in the Constitution, especially in Amendments 1–10 which are called the Bill of Rights. Among some of the main rights and freedoms outlined are:

- the right to vote
- the right to stand for election
- freedom of religion
- freedom of speech
- the right to protest and assembly
- the right to a fair trial

EQUALITY AND THE AMERICAN DREAM

Equality too is an important aspect of the American Dream. Everyone, it is said, has the same chances in life. They can go to school and college to be educated. They can get a good job and earn lots of money. Anyone, in theory, can start a business or buy a house.

Everyone in the US has, on the surface, the same opportunities as everyone else. Any American can become President or a film star according to the American Dream.

People may have left their own country because life was not very good there. These are often called *push factors*. The people were 'pushed' away.

The USA also seemed a good place to go to. The attractions of the USA are often called the *pull factors*. The people were 'pulled' to the USA.

Figure 4.2

Activities

1 Why do people go to live in the USA?

2 Using Figure 4.2 make up two spider diagrams to show the push factors and the pull factors which made people migrate to the USA. The first spider diagram has been started for you.

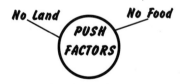

3 What is meant by the American Dream?

4 **"The USA is a Democratic Republic."**

What does this mean?

5 How can people participate in the US democratic system?

6 How can democracy help people to achieve the American Dream?

7 **"The US is a capitalist country."**

Using your own words explain what this means.

8 How can capitalism help Americans achieve the American Dream?

9 **"Equality is an important aspect of the American Dream."**

What does this mean?

10 **"The rights of people in the USA are an important aspect of the American Dream."**

What does this mean?

IMMIGRATION — THE MOOD TURNS SOUR.

At the border between the USA and Mexico, south of San Diego, a ten foot high fence has been built. It runs 14 miles from the Pacific coast into the desert. This is the line which divides Central and South America from the USA. On the Mexican side, poor people wait for patrols or curious sightseers to move on before they vault the fence or crawl through holes cut in the base. In other places they tie plastic bags around their feet and wade through the sewage in the Tijuana River. They are going to 'El Norte' to find work and improve their standards of living.

On the other side of the border, the border patrols wait to capture the migrants and return them to Mexico where they will try again.

Every night, somewhere along the US-Mexican border up to 2,000 illegal immigrants try to enter the US. Every night the immigration border patrols capture between 30% and 50% of them.

California is now home to an estimated 700,000 illegal immigrants from Mexico. Each year another 100,000 try to join them across the border.

However, many Californians are not happy. Some face competition for jobs from illegal immigrants. Steps are being taken to halt this immigration.

Proposition 187
In November 1994, Californians voted by 59% to 41% for Proposition 187 which is binding under law. Proposition 187 calls for an end to all publicly funded schooling for illegal immigrants, which means that about 300,000 children will be expelled from California classrooms. They will not go back to Mexico because their parents came to the USA to find work, so they will spend their days on the streets.

Proposition 187 also cuts off all welfare benefits and restricts health care to emergencies only. Up to 1994, California provided free natal care for pregnant women, including illegal immigrants. Their babies automatically become American citizens by birth which means that their mothers can claim $411 per month in cash and food stamps plus other benefits. Over 60% of the babies born in LA General Hospital were born to illegal immigrants.

The morning after the election, the State Governor issued an executive order directing health officials to stop providing ante-natal care to illegal immigrants. He claimed an immediate saving of $84 million. The education section of Proposition 187 is more difficult to implement. A 1982 Supreme Court ruling (Plyler v Doe) gave illegal immigrants the right to free public education. Therefore, applying Proposition 187 to the area of education will have to be examined by the Supreme Court to decide whether or not it is constitutional.

How they voted for Proposition 187 (%)		
Ethnic Group	Yes	No
White	64	36
Black	56	44
Hispanic	31	69
Asian	57	43

Table 4.2

Figure 4.3

BILL TO REDUCE IMMIGRATION

Opinion polls in the US consistently show that a majority of Americans oppose large-scale legal and illegal immigration. The Republicans introduced a bill into the House of Representatives in 1995 to reduce legal immigration by 30% from 800,000 to 500,000 per year. Other Republican members opposed the bill because it did not go far enough. They wanted all immigration ended while there was unemployment in the US.

Those opposed to immigration use a number arguments. These are summarised below.

- immigrants take jobs which could be done by unemployed US citizens

- immigrants work for lower wages and so undercut the wage rates of native born workers

- 1.8 million immigrants settled in the US in 1991—1 million entered illegally

- 6.6% of foreign born residents receive welfare benefits compared to 4.9% of native born citizens

- substantial numbers of elderly immigrants retire on federal benefits shortly after arriving in the US

- 25% of the federal prison population are foreign born

- 450,000 immigrants are in jail, on parole or on probation

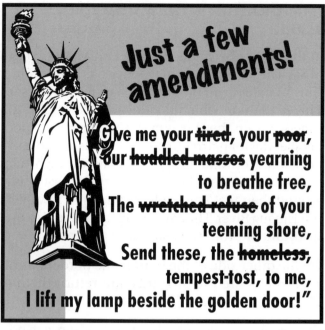

Just a few amendments!

"Give me all your ~~tired~~, your ~~poor~~, ~~our huddled masses~~ yearning to breathe free, The ~~wretched refuse~~ of your teeming shore, Send these, the ~~homeless~~, tempest-tost, to me, I lift my lamp beside the golden door!"

Figure 4.4

Activities

1 Why do people from Central and South America want to get into the USA?

2 How many illegal Mexican immigrants are in California and how many try to enter each year?

3 Why are Californians unhappy about this problem?

4 What is Proposition 187 and what was its effect on illegal immigrants living in California?

5 Study Figure 4.3.

   What point is the cartoonist trying to make about Proposition 187?

5 What other measures have been taken recently to reduce immigration to the USA?

6 What arguments do opponents of immigration use to support their point of view?

7 Imagine you are a Senator about to make a speech in opposition to a Bill stopping immigration. What arguments would you put forward?

8 Study Figure 4.4.

   What is the cartoonist trying to say about the American Dream?

What you will learn

1 What the US constitution is.
2 How the US government is organised.
3 How US citizens participate in the political system.
4 That women and ethnic groups are unfairly represented.
5 How people can participate in pressure group activities.

CONSTITUTION AND GOVERNMENT

A constitution is a set of rules which explains how the government of a country is meant to work. A constitution describes the structure of government, the types of laws the government can make, who are entitled to be part of the government and who are entitled to vote for the government.

In the UK we have an *unwritten* constitution. This means that there is no single document we can look up to find out how our government is meant to work.

The United States of America has a *written* constitution. This means that there is a document called a constitution which describes the government of the US and what that government is allowed to do. The US Constitution was signed in 1787.

Article 1 of the US Constitution describes how laws are made in the USA. It describes the work and membership of the House of Representatives and the Senate. It also describes what the government of the USA is entitled to make laws about.

Article 2 of the constitution describes the power of the President, who is entitled to hold the office of President and how long they are entitled to hold that office. Article 3 describes the power and membership of the Supreme Court of the United States.

In addition to the original constitution there are 27 amendments, the last of which was added in 1992. The first 10 amendments are known as the Bill of Rights because they protect the rights of the citizens of the United States from the power of the government. Amendment 1 guarantees freedom of speech and religion. Amendment 2 gives Americans the right to carry guns. Amendment 5 allows Americans the right to silence if they think their answers might incriminate them. Amendment 6 allows the citizens the right to a trial by jury.

THE GOVERNMENT OF THE USA

The constitution outlines the system of government in the USA. There are three branches of government.

The legislative branch: These are the people who make the laws. This is done by the Senate and the House of Representatives—collectively known as Congress. (The President is involved because he has to sign all bills before they become law.)

The executive branch: This consists of the people who carry out the laws which are made. The President and his staff are empowered to carry out the laws which are made by Congress.

The judicial branch: The judges determine whether a law passed is allowed by the constitution, ie. if it is constitutional, and whether or not people are guilty of breaking the law. This function is carried out by the Supreme Court.

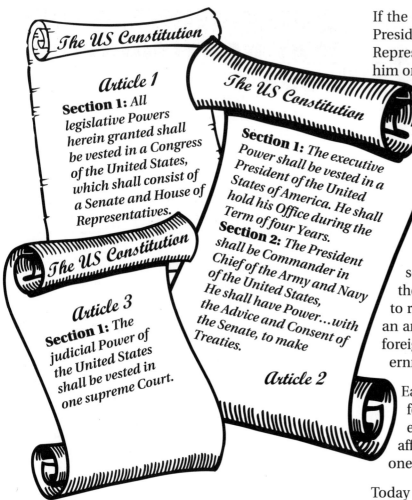

The US Constitution

Article 1

Section 1: All legislative Powers herein granted shall be vested in a Congress of the United States, which shall consist of a Senate and House of Representatives.

The US Constitution

Section 1: The executive Power shall be vested in a President of the United States of America. He shall hold his Office during the Term of four Years.

Section 2: The President shall be Commander in Chief of the Army and Navy of the United States, He shall have Power...with the Advice and Consent of the Senate, to make Treaties.

Article 2

The US Constitution

Article 3

Section 1: The judicial Power of the United States shall be vested in one supreme Court.

SEPARATION OF POWERS

Americans feel that there are dangers for the people if the three branches of government are concentrated in the hands of one person. In the US Constitution each branch of government was kept separate from the others.

The President and his office exercise the executive function. The Congress, which is split into two—the House of Representatives and the Senate—provides the legislative function. The judicial function is carried out by the Supreme Court.

For a bill to become a law in the USA it has to pass both Houses of Congress and be signed by the President. Even then it might not be accepted as a law if the Supreme Court says it is unconstitutional, ie. it is not allowed by the Constitution of the United States. Therefore each branch of government can act as a check on the power of the other two.

The timing of the elections was arranged so that the electorate could quickly change the balance of power should any group become dominant. Presidents are elected every 4 years. Representatives (Congressmen/women) are elected every 2 years. Senators are elected every 6 years, but every 2 years one-third of the Senate is up for election ie. about 33 Senators.

If the electorate are unhappy about the work of a President, after 2 years they can elect a House of Representatives and enough Senators to prevent him or her making laws they do not like. There are many checks and balances built into the constitution to prevent any one group from becoming too powerful.

STATE GOVERNMENT AND FEDERAL GOVERNMENT

When the United States gained its independence from Britain in 1783, it consisted of 13 independent colonies. To prevent themselves from going to war with each other over the ownership of the territories to the west, and to reduce the costs of each colony maintaining an army and a navy and having ambassadors in foreign countries, they decided to create one government for all of them.

Each state would keep the right to make laws for itself on internal matters, but a Federal government would be set up to deal with foreign affairs and matters which concerned more than one state or the country as a whole.

Today state governments have control over

- local laws eg. age of consent; age of compulsory education
- punishments eg. the form of capital punishment
- road provision
- local taxes

The Federal government has authority over

- the armed forces
- the post office
- the currency of the USA
- disputes between states
- foreign relations including declaring war and the negotiation of peace

POLITICAL PARTICIPATION – ELECTING THE PRESIDENT

According to the Constitution (Article 2, Section 1), the President of the USA has to be a natural born citizen, at least 35 years old and at least 14 years resident in the USA.

The term of office of a President is 4 years. Amendment 22 (1951) says that no person shall be elected President more than twice. The date of the Presidential election is fixed by law as the first Tuesday after the first Monday in November every leap year.

A US citizen can participate in the election of the President at several points in the process.

 A citizen can stand as a Presidential candidate. Very few choose to do so for a number of reasons, one of these being the cost involved in such a campaign.

 Some Americans may join their state political party—Democrats or Republicans. This entitles them to take part in the state primaries. Here they choose the person they want to be their party's candidate and also the state party's delegates to go to their party's national convention.

 If they are chosen as delegates to the national convention, they can participate by helping to choose their party's candidate for President.

 During the election campaign they can help their party's candidate by:
- handing out leaflets, stickers
- attending party campaign rallies
- telephoning voters to persuade them to vote for their candidate
- attending fundraising events

 On election day, people can participate by turning out to vote for their preferred candidate. Polling stations are open as early as 6 am in several states. The ballot is secret.

VOTE, VOTE, VOTE

The USA is a democracy. Electors in the USA are able to vote for many thousands of officials at city, county, state and federal levels. A single elector may be able to vote for up to 30 officials and representatives at one election.

In the County of Yolo in California, on 8 November 1994, the people had to vote for candidates for 15 posts. The electors were also asked to vote on propositions. These are issues on which the voters are asked to decide. If passed, these become state law.

Proposition 1 – buying railway rolling stock.

Proposition 2 – overturn a previous proposition.

Proposition 3 – the voting system in California.

Proposition 4 – increasing the sentences of convicted criminals.

Proposition 5 – petrol tax.

Activities

1 What is the purpose of the Constitution?

2 Give examples of some of the things that are in the US Constitution.

3 Draw a spider diagram to show the three branches of government in the US.

4 *"There are many checks and balances built into the constitution to prevent any one group from becoming too powerful."*

What are these checks and balances?

5 Describe the differences between the powers of the State Governments and the Federal Government.

6 According to the US Constitution

a) Who is allowed to be a candidate for President?

b) How long can one person serve as President?

c) When does a Presidential Election take place?

7 How can a US citizen participate in the election of a President?

8 *"The US is a very democratic country."*

With reference to voting in Yolo county, California, do you agree or disagree with this statement? Explain your answer.

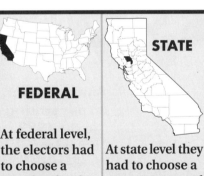

FEDERAL	STATE	YOLO COUNTY
At federal level, the electors had to choose a member for the House of Representatives and a United States Senator.	At state level they had to choose a state senator and a member of the state assembly. They also had to vote for members of the state supreme court. They voted for governor, lieutenant governor, state treasurer as well as 7 other state positions.	They might also have been asked to vote for the county sheriff, county coroner and county tax collector as well as the town mayor, the town dog catcher and the school board.

There are 2 ways to get a proposition on the ballot paper. Firstly, referendums can be placed on the ballot by state officials. Secondly, voter initiatives can be used. Voter initiatives must get a certain number of voter signatures to qualify for the ballot. Twenty four states in the USA allow such 'direct democracy'.

The Factfile below demonstrates that certain groups in the USA are unfairly represented. We will look at these groups now.

OTHER PARTIES

In the 1994 elections throughout the USA, there were candidates from 60 different political parties. In addition to the Democrats and Republicans some of these were:

Best Party	Damm Drug Dealers Party
Fed Up Party	Keep America First Party
People's Party	The Workers' League
Liberal Party	Socialist Workers' Party
Fascist Party	Green Party
Gun Control Party	Politicians are Crooks Party

FACTFILE: Electoral statistics

Are minorities fairly represented in the US political system?

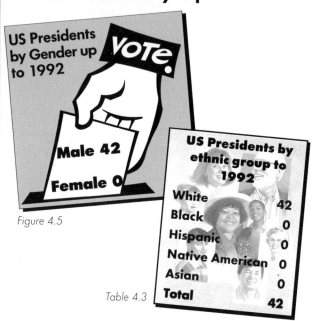

US Presidents by Gender up to 1992

Male 42
Female 0

Figure 4.5

US Presidents by ethnic group to 1992

White	42
Black	0
Hispanic	0
Native American	0
Asian	0
Total	42

Table 4.3

PROFILE OF THE 104TH CONGRESS (NOVEMBER 1994)

House of Representatives
- total 435 of which:
- 49 were women
- 39 were blacks
- 18 were Hispanics
- 6 were Asian/Pacific Islanders

Senate - total 100 of which:
- 8 were women
- 1 was black
- 2 were Asian/Pacific Islanders
- 1 was an American Indian

- There were only two black Republicans in Congress.
- Only one black person was elected to the Senate.
- In November 1992, the number of Hispanics increased from twelve to nineteen, and the number of Asian/Pacific Islanders from seven to eight, but in 1994, they made no gains.
- The most common religion is Roman Catholic, the average age is 52 and law is the most common occupation represented in Congress.

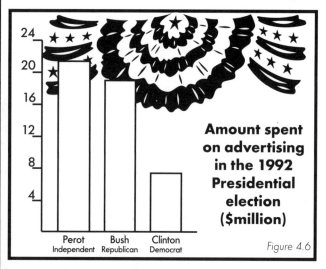

Amount spent on advertising in the 1992 Presidential election ($million)

Perot Independent — Bush Republican — Clinton Democrat

Figure 4.6

Presidential Election 1988 – Total Spending

DUKAKIS Democrat
BUSH Republican

($ million)   90   115

Figure 4.7

Examples of the money spent by Senators to win elections		
Barbara Boxer (D)	California 1992	$10.2 million
Phil Gramm (R)	Texas 1990	$9.8 million
Bill Bradley (D)	New Jersey 1990	$9.5 million
Alfonse D'Amato (R)	New York 1992	$9.1 million

Table 4.4

Of the 50 Senators who were elected in 1990 or 1992, only 3 Senators spent less than $1 million on their campaign. The 'cheapest' campaign was by Thad Cochran the Republican Senator for Mississippi who spent 'only' $567,446.

In 1994, Michael Huffington spent $20 million of his own wealth on advertising trying to become a senator for California.

MINORITIES IN CONGRESS 1992 & 1994

	House		Senate		Total	
	1992	1994	1992	1994	1992	1994
Women	48	49	6	8	54	57
Blacks	39	39	1	1	40	40
Hispanics	19	18	0	0	19	18
Asian & Pacific Islanders	7	6	2	2	9	8
American Indian	0	0	1	1	1	1

Table 4.5

WOMEN

Since 1990, the number of women in the Senate has quadrupled from two to eight. Five of these are Democrats and three are Republicans. In the House, women gained one seat giving them a total of 49. In the 1988 Congress the number of women increased from 29 to 48.

Although women make up 51% of the population and 53% of the voters, they only make up 13% of the membership of Congress, 8% of state governors and 21% of state legislators.

There are a number of reasons why so few women become representatives. Firstly, they do not put themselves forward as candidates. The traditional role of wife, mother and homemaker is very strong in many parts of the United States. This discourages women from participating.

Secondly, it is argued that the political system is biased in favour of those already in office and most of those in office are men. As long as they run for re-election, it is difficult for any outsider—male or female—to win.

Women have been making progress in recent years. The figures show a significant increase in the number of women in Congress between 1988 and 1992. Nevertheless, it is still well short of the 51% of women in the population as a whole.

BLACKS AND HISPANICS

Blacks and Hispanics made great gains in the 1992 elections to Congress. This was mainly due to the 1986 Supreme Court interpretation of the Voting Rights Act which says that minorities must be given maximum opportunity to elect people from their own group to Congress.

In thirteen states, boundaries were redrawn specifically to elect new minority members. This made it possible for thirteen new blacks and six new Hispanics to be elected to the House of Representatives. For the first time since the middle of the nineteenth century, the House had black members from Alabama, Florida, North Carolina, South Carolina and Virginia. In 1994 there were forty blacks and eighteen Hispanics in Congress. The number of blacks and Hispanics in Congress increased in 1992 and remained almost as high in 1994.

There has been a significant increase in the number of ethnic minority candidates elected at state or city level throughout the US (see table 4.6).

BLACK ELECTED OFFICIALS

	US & State Legislatures	City & County Offices	Law Enforcement	Education	Total
1970	182	715	213	362	1,472
1980	326	2,382	526	1,206	4,980
1990	447	4,499	769	1,655	7,370
1993	571	4,825	923	1,694	8,016

Table 4.6

More seats less influence?

It would appear that the power and influence of ethnic minority groups is increasing. In certain areas this may be true, but, in fact, the increased number of ethnic minority members of Congress may paradoxically lead to a reduction of interest in minority issues.

By concentrating larger numbers of the ethnic minorities in certain electoral areas, they will be represented by fewer Congressmen/women. Therefore, there will be fewer Congressmen/women interested in the issues which affect the minorities. So in the House of Representatives, more Congressmen/women from the minorities may lead other Congressmen/women to lose interest in the problems of the minority groups.

ASIAN AND PACIFIC ISLANDERS

Eight Asian and Pacific Islanders were elected as members of Congress in 1994. Traditionally the Asian community has remained isolated within American society and has not participated in the political system. This is now slowly changing and more Asians are standing as candidates. The Pacific Islander representatives in Congress mainly come from Hawaii.

NATIVE AMERICANS

The only Native American in the Senate is Ben Nighthorse Campbell. He was elected to the Senate in 1992. His arrival in the Senate, along with the seven newly elected women senators, was seen as a victory for the many under-represented people in the USA. Until then, the two million Native Americans had a poor record of participation in national politics, mainly due to apathy fuelled by poverty and unemployment. In 1992, many Native Americans were coaxed to vote. Reservations were bombarded with mailshots and telephone calls to get the voters to turn out. Ben Nighthorse Campbell also won the support of trade unions, ranchers and Hispanics to enable him to be elected.

Activities

1 Draw a bar chart showing the increase in the number of women in the House of Representatives from 1988 to 1994.

2 Does the increase shown in the bar chart mean that women are now fairly represented in the House of Representatives? Justify your answer.

3 Why do so few women become representatives?

4 Why has the number of blacks and Hispanics in Congress increased?

5 Using the Factfile on page 74, explain why poor people might find it difficult to be elected in the USA?

6 Who are most likely to vote?

Compare the turnout for:

- males/females

- ethnic groups

7 What happens to turnout as people get older?

8 Does education have an effect on turnout?

9 Does employment affect turnout?

TURNOUT

CHARACTERISTICS OF VOTERS IN THE 1992 PRESIDENTIAL ELECTION IN THE USA

The table and graphs below show the percentage of voters who said that they did vote in the 1992 Presidential Election.

The percentage who voted by level of education

Level of education	Percentage
8 years or less	30.3%
9–11 years	41.2%
12 years	57.5%
16+ years	81.5%

Figure 4.8 Level of education of voters

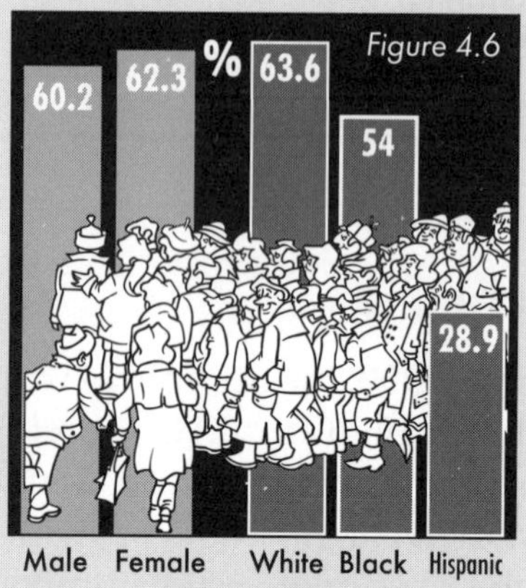

Figure 4.6

	%
Male	60.2
Female	62.3
White	63.6
Black	54
Hispanic	28.9

Table 4.7

Age Group	Percentage who voted
18–20	38.5
21–24	45.7
25–34	53.2
35–44	63.6
45–54	68.8
55–64	71.6
65–74	73.8
75+	64.8

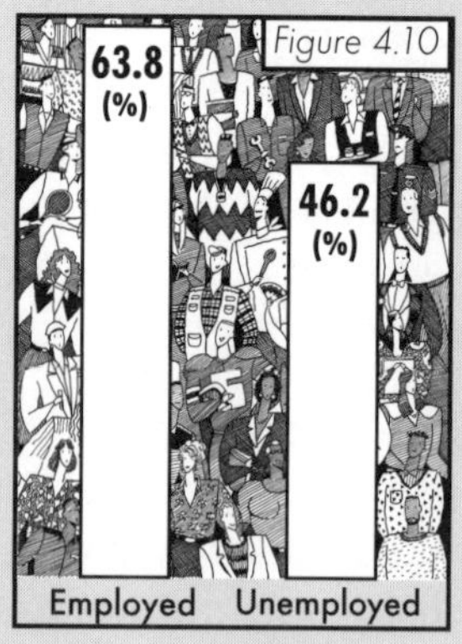

Figure 4.10

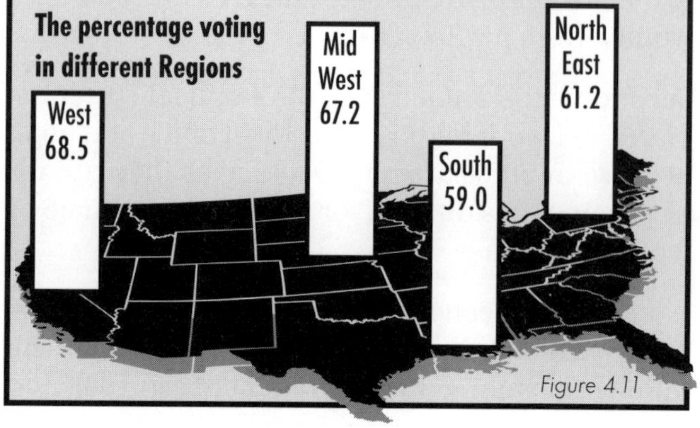

Employed	Unemployed
63.8 (%)	46.2 (%)

The percentage voting in different Regions

Region	Percentage
West	68.5
Mid West	67.2
South	59.0
North East	61.2

Figure 4.11

WHY SOME PEOPLE DO NOT VOTE

LOW VOTER REGISTRATION

Before you can vote in the USA you must be registered to vote (except in North Dakota where voters do not have to register). Each state has its own voter registration procedure.

For the 1994 elections to Congress, 67.2% of the US voting age population was registered to vote. This had increased from 65.2% in 1990. Mississippi had the highest figure with 87% of the population registered to vote; Hawaii and South Carolina had the lowest with 54%. Voter registration among young people rose by 10% to 68% between 1992 and 1994.

Why might voter registration be low?

1   The registration procedure can be complicated. Some American citizens may not have the educational ability to complete the appropriate forms. This may be linked to ethnic background since many blacks and Hispanics do not have the same opportunities at school as some whites do.

2   Some groups in American society feel that voting is a waste of time because, even if their choice of candidate wins the election, life does not necessarily improve for them. Some of these people will, therefore, not bother to register to vote as they see no benefit in it for them.

3   In some rural areas it may be difficult to get to the registration office. This means that many poorer Americans will not register to vote.

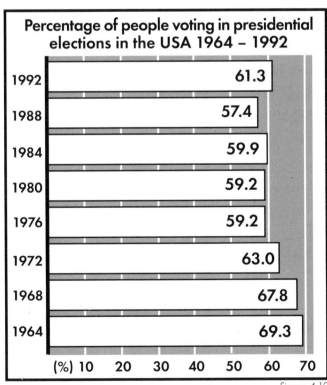

Percentage of people voting in presidential elections in the USA 1964 – 1992

Year	%
1992	61.3
1988	57.4
1984	59.9
1980	59.2
1976	59.2
1972	63.0
1968	67.8
1964	69.3

Figure 4.12

LOW VOTER TURNOUT (PARTICIPATION)

Voter turnout is affected by whether or not it is a Presidential election year. Figure 4.13 shows that for both blacks and whites there is a significantly higher turnout in Presidential election years than for mid-term elections.

For example in 1988, a Presidential election year, white turnout was 59%, but the following mid-term elections in 1990 saw the turnout fall to 48%. Black turnout in 1988 was 51% but in 1990 it fell to 39%. In the 1990 mid-term elections only 33% of all voters voted.

Voter turnout, therefore, is affected by whether or not a President is being elected. The TV coverage of the process of electing a President obviously increases voter awareness and interest. There is significantly less interest in only electing a Congressman/woman or state officials.

Bottom 5 Voter turnouts: 1994	
South Carolina	34.12%
Mississippi	32.60%
West Virginia	31.64%
Georgia	29.95%
Kentucky	27.45%

Table 4.8

The low turnout can be explained also by a combination of other factors. Firstly, many elections are held for many different posts and people can be put off voting because it happens so often. Secondly, the registration form can be long and complicated and is, itself, a barrier to registering for some people. Thirdly, the ballot paper is often long and complicated and some voters may find it confusing.

Fourthly, voting may not be seen to improve people's lives and so they do not vote. For example, many blacks and Hispanics have poor life chances. They live in poor areas of the city where standards of living are low. Schools often provide inferior education and the dropout rate is high. There is a high level of unemployment and this can lead to crime and prostitution. Housing is often substandard and people's health is poor. These factors help to explain why many blacks and Hispanics are not interested in voting since they see it as having no direct relevance to their lives.

Finally, many Hispanics are illegal immigrants and so do not qualify, under the Constitution, to vote.

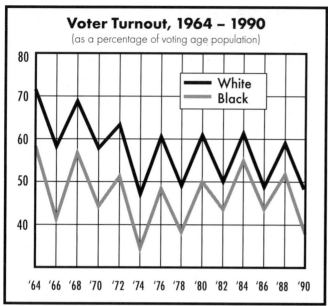

Voter Turnout, 1964 – 1990
(as a percentage of voting age population)

Figure 4.13

Figure 4.13 illustrates a number of points. Firstly, between 1964 and 1990 white turnout has always been higher than black turnout. Secondly, the gap between the turnout figures for blacks and whites narrowed between 1964 and 1986 when the difference was down to 3.8%. Blacks were turning out to vote in larger numbers because of voter registration campaigns and the increasing number of black candidates standing for election.

In 1988 and 1990 the trend seems to be reversing. Figures for 1992 also suggest that the gap between the turnout of black and white voters was widening. The measures taken by Reagan and Bush which adversely affected the minorities might have led to disillusion with the electoral system and to reduced turnout. There is also evidence that there is less priority placed on voter registration campaigns. Sonia Jarvis of The National Coalition on Black Voter Participation claimed that, "candidates and parties are not placing enough emphasis on voter registration and education."

Lastly, it shows that, overall, there was a downward trend in the turnout of both blacks and whites between 1964 and 1990.

Black voter discontent

GM SMITH, a longtime resident of Los Angeles, voted for Bill Clinton in 1992, thinking that a new administration would bring him a better job and a safer environment. He is still doing odd jobs and worries that he will not be able to look after his new baby properly.

Mr Smith and his wife, Karen, said they will not be voting this year because they are disappointed in President Clinton and have been put off by campaigning TV adverts in which candidates seem to talk about nothing but locking up criminals. Many blacks have been alienated by the Democrat policies on crime and welfare. They say that as they watch their suburbs fall into neglect, they have no patience for the new tough lines on crime which many interpret as anti-black.

Mr and Mrs Smith complained that no-one was trying to persuade them to vote. "It took us black people so long to get the vote," said Mr Smith. "Now, they're making us not want to vote. What politicians offer us blacks is no good to us."

Activities

1 Give 2 reasons to explain why voter registration might be low.

2 From Figure 4.12, describe the trends in US Presidential election voter turnout between 1964 and 1992.

3 Explain why there is a lower turnout at mid-term elections compared to Presidential election years.

4 What other reasons may explain low voter turnout?

5 Why did the gap in voter turnout between blacks and whites narrow between 1964 and 1986?

6 What has happened to this trend since 1986? Why is this?

7 Why has GM Smith decided no longer to turn out to vote?

8 What other reasons can be given for lower black and Hispanic turnout?

POLITICAL PARTICIPATION – PRESSURE GROUP ACTIVITIES

In the USA there are many different types of pressure groups which are usually called interest groups. People can participate in these interest groups in a number of ways. Here is an example of how an interest group can try to get things changed.

In California in 1994, an interest group, called *Californians for Statewide Smoking Restrictions,* campaigned to get a proposition put on the November ballot. (A proposition or voter initiative, if passed by the voters, directly changes the law of the State. Often a proposition is put on a ballot paper because of the actions of an interest group.) The proposition, called the California Uniform Tobacco Control Act, sought to impose "tough smoking restrictions in more that 200 localities that currently have no regulations at all."

To get the proposition on the ballot paper the interest group had to get 600,000 people to sign a petition. Members of the interest group either telephoned or wrote to registered voters asking them to sign the petition. The voters were given information about what the proposition would mean. (See Figure 4.14)

The interest group was successful in getting the proposition on the ballot paper because it had involved people in a number of ways.

- ℂ By a telephone campaign. Supporters of the interest group telephoned people to persuade them to sign the petition.

- ✉ By a mailing campaign. Supporters of the interest group sent letters persuading people to support them.

- ✉ Leaflets and posters were distributed throughout California.

- ❝❞ Campaign rallies were held where people could hear all the arguments put forward to support the proposition.

- ⚏ The interest group used the media to get support for its campaign. TV and radio time was bought by the interest group and used to persuade the public to support their campaign. Adverts were placed in newspapers like *The Los Angeles Times.*

- ☞ Campaign supporters lobbied members of Congress.

Figure 4.14

LOBBYING

Interest groups operate either through general campaigns to persuade the public or through direct contacts with members of Congress.

This direct contact with members of Congress is called *lobbying.* Lobbying takes place in Washington DC at Congress. A Washington lobby group uses the methods it sees as appropriate for the circumstances.

- ● *Bribery* was used frequently in the 19th and early 20th centuries. However, after the Second World War, this direct vote-buying by lobbyists was replaced, for the most part, by more sophisticated techniques.

- ● *Campaign support* – Interest groups can give campaign contributions to members of Congress. This might encourage a Congressman/woman to back the pressure groups' interests in Congress as well as ensuring that Congressmen/women who support these groups remain in office.

- *Grass-roots pressure* – During a lobby campaign, an interest group will mobilise the public to support its case. For the most part, citizens are urged to contact their members of Congress in support of or in opposition to a particular bill. The National Rifle Association (NRA) is a good example of a successful grass-roots lobbying group. It is large, well-organised and concentrates on a single issue.

- *Direct lobbying* – Much lobbying is conducted on a face-to-face basis. An interest group can provide a senator with much of the research needed for a speech on a particular topic. This is a valuable service to many because members of the party which does not control the White House cannot use the research services of the departments as much as other members can.

- *Testimony at Congressional hearings* – Another useful technique for lobbyists is testimony at Congressional hearings. This gives the interest group access to key members of Congress. Lobbyists try to ensure a large turnout of supporters on the hearing day.

CASE STUDY – ABORTION

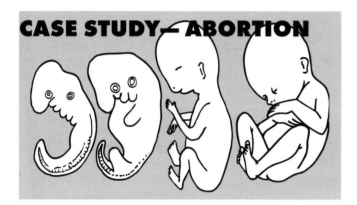

Abortion has been a major political issue in the USA since it was first made legal in 1970. The debate is between liberals who argue that it is a woman's right to choose whether to have a child or not and those on the political right wing who believe that abortion is wrong because it kills unborn babies, upsets 'family values' or it will cost the taxpayer money.

In 1973, the Supreme Court ruled that women had the right to choose whether or not to have an abortion in consultation with their doctor. However, there are some problems which may be encountered by women trying to exercise that right. Until the Freedom of Choice Act of 1992, abortions were illegal under state law in states like Louisiana and Utah. Other states required married women to notify their husbands of their intention to have an abortion.

Another major problem is the lack of a nationally available health care system in the USA. Access to clinics willing to perform abortions is therefore very patchy and is particularly poor in rural areas, the southern states and the mid-west. President Bush issued a decree that federally funded birth control clinics could not discuss abortion and there was legislation to prevent federal funds from being spent on abortions.

Safe abortion is therefore effectively unavailable to the poor in the USA and is only patchily available in rural America. Abortion is essentially available only to rich or middle-class women who live in urban areas or who can travel to private clinics in these areas and who can afford to pay the insurance premiums to have the operation done privately.

THE MAIN PLAYERS

Pro-abortion or pro-choice groups:

- Planned Parenthood Federation

Anti-abortion or pro-life groups:

- Rescue Outreach
- Rescue America
- Operation Rescue
- The Christian Coalition (mainly white Protestant Republicans)
- National Right to Life
- Priests for Life (Catholic priests)

The main aims

The anti-abortionists want abortion to become illegal once more in the USA, except where a woman's life is in danger. The pro-abortion groups seek to defend a woman's right to choose and to improve access to clinics so that the right to choose is not thwarted by the unavailability of facilities.

Tactics employed

> It may be necessary "to intervene physically with violence" because "that is the logical response to murder and abortion is murder."
>
> (Randall Terry, founder of the anti-abortion movement)

The anti-abortionists employed all the usual pressure group tactics, but some of the more extreme groups like *Operation Outreach* and *Operation Rescue* organised some extreme forms of *direct action.*

✳ Threatening phone calls to opponents and to doctors and nurses who work in the clinics.

✳ Phone call campaigns to right-wing radio talk shows. These are hosted by 'shock-jocks' who peddle half-truths, incite their audience to violence eg. tell them how to shoot people and generally abuse liberals, foreigners, homosexuals, government officials etc. Surveys show that most callers are white, male and right wing.

✳ Photograph the staff at the clinics, blow up the photographs and put these on wanted posters.

✳ Picketing or laying siege to abortion clinics with the aim of preventing women from entering the clinic or else closing it down.

WANTED

For killing babies

DEAD OR ALIVE

✳ Occupation of abortion clinics

✳ Vandalism against clinics doubled between 1991 and 1992.

✳ Arson increased threefold between 1990 and 1993.

✳ Arson has now been replaced by spraying these clinics with butyric acid which smells foul and makes the staff ill. Clinics need to be closed and redecorated after such attacks.

✳ 12 March 1993 – An anti-abortionist demonstrator named Michael Griffith shot and killed Dr David Gunn outside a clinic.

✳ December 1994 – An abortion clinic in Brookline, Massachusetts, was sprayed with gunfire. Two workers were killed and five others were injured.

Anti-abortionists are encouraged by the fact that law and order is a matter for the local police and judges reflect local opinion which is often fiercely anti-abortion.

Effectiveness?

The campaign and its tactics have certainly kept the issue to the fore in US politics for over 25 years. Pressure has led to:

● debates and legal argument in state legislatures and in the federal House of Representatives and Senate

● the introduction of legislation in Congress and in a number of state assemblies

● the Supreme Court passing a number of judgments on existing laws and various connected cases which have come before it

● whether a candidate is pro or anti abortion now being an important question which is asked of anyone seeking office at state or federal level and in the appointment of judges and other officials

● the outcome of several elections in various parts of the US being influenced.

The killing of Dr Gunn and the other murders has probably been counterproductive. The Catholic Church has distanced itself from these tactics while still opposing abortion. States have been forced by federal legislation to drop their anti-abortion laws. Despite an upsurge in electoral support for the right-wing Republican Party, it appears that the right of women to have a choice is secure, but the right to have access to facilities which enable women to exercise that choice appears to be a long way off.

Activities

1 What do Americans call pressure groups?

2 How did the interest group *Californians for Statewide Smoking Restrictions* gain support for their campaign?

3 What is lobbying?

4 What methods are used by lobby groups in the USA?

5 Which interest groups were involved in the argument over abortion in the USA and what were the aims of these groups?

6 Some of these groups used direct action tactics. Give some examples of the direct action used.

7 Make up a table with 2 headings:

Appropriate forms of direct action
Inappropriate forms of direct action

For all forms of action used put them under one of these headings.

8 How effective have these campaigns been?

What you will learn

1 Americans have rights written into their constitution.

2 Americans have the right to carry guns.

3 With rights should come responsibilities.

THE ISSUE OF GUNS IN THE USA

It is your right, according to the constitution, to own a gun in the USA. However, by law, in most states, it is your responsibility to display and use a gun only in your own home or place of business. It is obvious that many Americans feel the need to carry guns despite the possibility of tragic consequences. It makes people feel safer as they can protect themselves.

In 1996, Texas, following the example of Florida, passed a law allowing citizens to carry concealed weapons. One of the sponsors of the Bill, Democrat state Representative Ron Wilson stated, "All I want to do is put innocent people, those who are potential victims, in a position of being able to protect themselves." Opponents fear that the law will unleash more violence on the streets and return Texas to its Wild West roots.

THE NATIONAL RIFLE ASSOCIATION (NRA)

Emblem of the NRA

The membership of the NRA in the mid-1990s stood at 3.3 million with a growing proportion of females in their ranks. Amid fears of national violence following the Los Angeles riots in May 1992, the NRA's membership increased by 1,500 *per day* for a short time. Californians bought a record 20,578 guns in the first eleven days of May 1992. Recently membership figures have tailed off, perhaps as a result of the Clinton Administration's anti-gun stance.

In 1993 Congress passed the Brady Bill, named after Jim Brady, Ronald Reagan's press secretary, who was shot in the head during an assassination attempt on the former President. This federal measure imposes a five-day waiting period on the purchase of handguns and requires the police to check on the background and suitability of would-be buyers. In early 1995, however, President Clinton failed to get Congressional approval for a federal bill prohibiting the sale of other types of semi-automatic weapons.

Easy to get a gun in the USA

IN THE state of Vermont, any 'law-abiding' 21-year-old with a driving licence can buy a gun. There is no waiting period and no investigation into personal history.

I decided to find out if they would sell me a gun—a female who knows nothing about guns.

In Woolworths, I discovered they would. The guy in the sports department told me that Woolworths no longer sold hand guns but he gave me advice. He recommended a .25 calibre gun. It cost about £70 new.

I then tried a dim, musty basement shop which only sold guns. It sold all sorts of guns—from machine guns to sawn-off shotguns. Here I was given several hand guns to try. Picking up a Lorcin Model .25 calibre, I could hardly move the slide to load the magazine. What a pity! The chrome finish with pink bits would have gone nicely with my new dress!

I asked about buying a gun. I was given a registration form. The shopkeeper said, "If you answer YES to any of these questions, I can't sell you a gun." I said no to them all! OK, so I lied once or twice. Who is to know? So, is it easy to get a gun in the USA—YES it is!

(Adapted from *The Scotsman* 11 March 1993)

FACTFILE: Guns

1. 45% of all households across the USA have at least one firearm.

2. The number of licensed gun dealers in the USA has risen from 150,000 to 284,000 in the past twenty years. You do not need a federal licence to sell ammunition.

3. While most guns used in criminal activity are semi-automatic handguns (guns which require the user to squeeze the trigger for each bullet), semi-automatic rifles are increasingly being converted to allow automatic fire. The result is, in effect, a machine gun which is banned by federal law.

4. Being shot by a hand gun is the second highest cause of death for high school children.

5. In 1991 there were over 12,000 handgun suicides in the USA—one in five of these by a child or teenager using the parental gun. A handgun, statistics show, is 64 times more likely to kill or wound a family member than an unauthorised intruder.

6. In Los Angeles schools in 1993, more than 400 firearms were confiscated—pupils can buy a small pistol nicknamed a 'Saturday Night Special' for as little as £40.

7. In Thomas Jefferson High School in New York, which has the reputation of being the most violent in the country and where the doors are steel plated, more than seventy students have been seriously hurt as a result of guns in the past four years.

Body Count
Number of homicides by year

Year	Number
1970	16,000
1975	20,510
1980	23,040
1985	18,980
1990	23,440
1993	24,500

Table 4.9

In most states anyone over 17 can legally buy a handgun. Convicted felons (criminals) are not legally meant to own a firearm.

Number of homicides per 100,000 people

The murder rate peaked in 1980 at 10.2 per 100,000

Figure 4.15

Deaths involving firearms (1990)

	Homicides	Suicide	Total
Male	13,629	16,285	31,455
Female	2,589	2,600	5,408
Total	16,218	18,885	36,866

Table 4.10

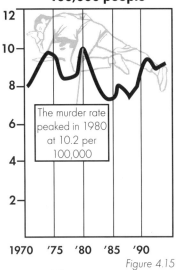

Of the 23,440 homicides in 1990, 70% (16,218) were caused by a firearm.

The most common cause of death among black men aged between 15 and 25 is homicide.

Over half of the murders in the USA—56%—are caused by blacks. Over half of the murder victims in the USA—51%—are black. Blacks mostly kill blacks and whites mostly kill whites.

WHAT THEY SAY ABOUT THE NRA AND GUN CONTROL

"If everyone has a gun, nobody will risk using one. Gun control not only leaves the law-abiding citizen defenceless but also represents a subversion of the freedoms that America is supposed to stand for." (NRA supporter)

"A well-regulated militia being necessary to the security of the state, the right of the people to keep and bear arms shall not be infringed."
(4th Amendment to the USA Constitution.)

"Guns are a great leveller; they put the powerful at the mercy of any pauper with arms."

"The NRA would have you believe that the only people who buy guns are the great outdoors types who hunt bears in the Rockies. Why then do so many Americans buy guns to shoot each other?"

"Gun laws are so lax in most states, the only thing you need to buy a gun is a credit card."
(Mel Fryer, American Liberal Journalist)

"Gun ownership…increases the risk of your being shot. In most cases the people who get hit are not the people you are aiming at but your own children, your neighbours, your husband, yourself."
(Senator Charles Schumer)

Activities

1   Use the information on Rights and Freedoms on page 67 to answer the following:

   a) What is the Bill of Rights?

   b) Complete the table below.

Rights	Responsibilities linked to these Rights
Right to vote	Go out and vote

2   What gives citizens of the USA the right to carry guns?

3   In most states what responsibilities do you have if you own a gun?

4   What is the NRA?

5   Why did membership of the NRA increase in the early 1990s?

6   How easy is it to buy a gun in the USA? Give evidence to support your answer.

7   Using all the information in this section, imagine you live in an American state which is about to put the issue of gun ownership to its citizens in a referendum (a 'yes' or 'no' vote).

   EITHER make up a speech and/or poster to persuade citizens that the use and sale of guns should be banned. Give reasons for your point of view.

   OR make up a speech and/or poster to persuade citizens that guns should be legal and openly on sale to adults in your state. Give reasons for your point of view.

8   ***"Citizens in the USA do not use guns responsibly."*** (Viewpoint of a US Senator)

   Using all of the information in the Guns Factfile write a report supporting the viewpoint.

What you will learn

1   Certain groups face social inequalities.
2   Certain groups face economic inequalities.
3   Why these groups face social and economic inequalities.
4   What Affirmative Action is and how effective it has been.

In this section we will look at the Social and Economic issues facing different groups in US society.

Social issues
- education
- health
- housing
- crime
- racial disharmony

Economic issues
- unemployment
- poverty

"BROKEN DREAMS, DRUGS AND GUNFIRE"

The following are excerpts adapted from an article about life in Washington Heights, a New York neighbourhood. In 1991 there were 122 murders in Washington Heights, with at least 12 of these on one street alone—West 162nd Street.

- About 5,000 people live on the street, most of them struggling to survive. They came with expectation and live with despair.

- "It was heaven here," Mr Jennings said. "You could walk the street at 3 in the morning whistling a tune and nobody would bother you. Today if you try that you're dead."

- West 162nd Street is a place where too many people live on too little income, where there are too many teenagers with too little to do, where there are too many drug dealers and too many senseless killings, where there is too much rumbling about how something must be done that falls on too many unhearing ears.

- "They are mostly very hard-working decent people who live on this block," said a young Hispanic woman. "They all scrimp and save and dream of a better day. And then there is the trouble element who deals the drugs and plays cowboy on the street."

- Up to the 1950s, mostly working-class immigrants from Europe lived on the street. After the Second World War, Puerto Ricans and some Dominicans settled in the area. By the 1960s, Puerto Ricans, Cubans and blacks dominated the street. As these people moved to the suburbs, they were replaced by Dominican immigrants who jam-packed apartments. Now Dominicans make up more than half of the population. Many of them hold blue-collar jobs with low wages or collect Public Assistance (social security). The median income is about $20,000 per year. A third of the residents are below the poverty line.

- 28% of all households in West 162nd Street received Public Assistance in 1989.

- Drug dealing has reached epidemic proportions on the street.

- Death is a regular visitor to the street. Painted on the side of 505 is a black and grey mural of a cemetery. Listed on it are the names of dead from the neighbourhood, 51 in all. There is space for plenty more.

- Genela Sanchez came to the USA from Santo Domingo and has lived on West 162nd Street for 10 years. "The neighbourhood was once nice and tranquil. All that is now gone. Every time I walk out of my apartment, I'm scared and nervous. I have sent my daughters back to Santo Domingo to be raised by their aunts. It is too dangerous here for them." For herself, she can't leave. She feels she is too accustomed to the American way of life.

- Many people came to West 162nd Street brimming with hope and many have had the last drop siphoned out of them.

POPULATION CHANGE ON WEST 162ND STREET

Year	Hispanic	White	Black	Others
1950	5.1	63.3	31.4	0.2
1960	10.4	54.1	26.4	0.6
1970	41.0	24.0	33.7	1.8
1980	57.6	8.0	31.7	8.0
1990	70.0	5.1	22.7	5.1

Table 4.11

In a filthy single room at the back of a drinking den in South Central Los Angeles lives Tom, a 60-year-old alcoholic. He lives with his 'friend' Tina. She is 17 and has been addicted to alcohol since the age of 11. This is the USA in the 1990s. They live in squalid conditions just half an hour's car ride from Beverly Hills, the home of the rich and famous. A recent survey of US inner cities reported that black males living in places like Harlem (NY) or Watts (LA) have less chance of reaching 40 years old than they would if they lived in Bangladesh.

Activities

1 Under the heading *Economic Problems* identify the main economic problems facing people in Washington Heights.

2 Under the heading Social Problems identify the main social problems facing people in Washington Heights.

3 Explain why the article opposite is called Third World USA.

CRIME AND JUSTICE IN THE USA

When crack moved in, the people moved out

JACKSONVILLE, Florida is not unique. Downtown Jacksonville in the 1980s was the focal point for the black middle class. Now it is desolate. The people moved out when the crack moved in.

In Jacksonville, as in most US cities, the crack population is an aging one and crack is past its peak, but its effects are still there. The Jacksonville narcotics unit spends 75% of its time on crack cases. Children born to crack addicted mothers are just starting school. Perhaps 3 out of every 100 children are in this category. Most of these children have a low intelligence level and may need special classes, which are expensive.

Crack has also hit the local medical system. Crack has brought two big burdens to Jacksonville hospitals. It has led to an increase in gunshot wounds and other injuries as crack dealers defend their areas. The other is crack-related medical problems such as heart conditions, dam-

aged babies and sexually transmitted diseases. Most of the people in these categories are uninsured so the community has to fund the high cost of treatment.

For the average person living in Jacksonville, the most obvious effect of crack is crime. Violent crime is 6 times worse in downtown Jacksonville that it is in the rest of the city. Both the jail and the morgue have been greatly expanded in recent years. Downtown Jacksonville is almost entirely black, although many crack users are white. (Bureau of Justice statistics 49.9% of crack users are white, 35.9% are black, 14.2% are Hispanic.)

Homicides – 1991 a record year

IN Youngstown, Ohio, 2 teenage girls were arguing over a boyfriend when one of them fatally shot the other with a pistol. The 17-year-old was Youngstown's 58th homicide in 1991, up from 19 in 1990.

In Little Rock, Arkansas, a 15-year-old boy driving a stolen car got angry with a pedestrian and shot him. So far there have been 51 homicides, up from 34 last year.

So far in 1991, more than a dozen US cities have reported record levels of homicides. Those include 3 of the USA's largest 10 cities—Dallas, Phoenix, San Diego—as well as places such as Milwaukee, Jackson, Mississippi, New Haven, Connecticut, Chattanooga, Tennessee, Colorado Springs, Charlotte, North Carolina and Rochester, New York.

It is thought that the increase in the drug trade is the main cause of the increase in violence. For example, in Youngstown the increase in murders is directly related to the spread of crack cocaine.

(Adapted: *The Herald Tribune* December 1991)

Arrests of different ethnic groups for selected crimes in the USA, 1991

Whites
Blacks
Others*

Burglary
2%
29%
68%

Murder
2%
55%
43%

Robbery
1%
61%
38%

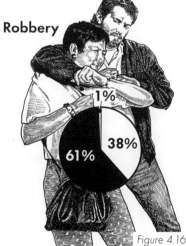

(* 'Others' includes Native Americans and Asian Americans)

Figure 4.16

GANGS – AN AMERICAN TRADITION

GANGS HAVE LONG BEEN a feature of American life. Since the late 1800s teenagers, usually poor male immigrants, have banded together in US cities. Gangs have entered US culture in novels, films like *The Wild One* and even a musical, *West Side Story*. A survey carried out by the National Institute of Justice in 1992 found out that the police knew of 5,000 gangs with 250,000 members in the USA's 79 biggest cities. Two Los Angeles gangs, the Bloods and the Crips, are household names.

Today, gangs are a source of fear in many urban areas of the US. There are many places where gunfire is a steady background noise; where school closes when guns are fired; where children are dressed with care each morning because the wrong colours could make them targets and are put to sleep under their beds some nights because stray bullets are less likely to get them there.

A possible solution to the gang problem in the USA would be to try to improve the life chances of young, especially black, men. This would seem to be a good solution but it is largely in the hands of the politicians. However, in Chicago, for example, gang members are now taking part in politics.

Activities

1   What differences are there between ethnic groups and types of crime? (figure 4.16)

2   There has been a significant increase in the homicide (murder) rate among young people in US cities.
    Give two reasons which might explain this increase.

3   i) How big is the gang problem in US cities? Use the figures to support your answer.

    ii) How do gangs affect the lives of people in US cities?

4   According to the American Dream *"all people are equal before the law."*
    Using the information in this section, decide whether this is true or not. Explain your answer using examples.

5   Between 1960 and 1990 the number of lawyers in the USA increased by nearly 300%. Can you explain this? (Think about money.)

Are all people equal before the law?

OJ SIMPSON, the black sports and film star, was accused of killing his ex-wife, Nicole, and her friend Ron Goldman on 13 June 1993 in Los Angeles. Both victims were white. It is thought that if Simpson had been poor and unknown the trial would have all been over in 2 days—an open and shut case, but OJ Simpson could afford to pay for the best defence. It is estimated that on the day of his arrest he was worth $10 million. According to one of his lawyers, he spent $5–6 million by the end of the trial. It was money well spent because he was found not guilty.

The Simpson case demonstrated that money changes everything. Paul Petterson, a defence coordinator in the USA said, "There are 2 criminal justice systems in this country. There is a whole different system for poor people. It's in the same courthouse—it's not separate but it's not equal."

In South Central LA—a poor black area with jobless rates of 50% among teenagers—most people questioned said

OJ Simpson spent over $5 million to defend himself.

that OJ Simpson was framed or targeted because of racism. "His wife turned up dead and they pointed the finger at him because he's a black man with a white woman," said one LA citizen. Opinion polls showed that most whites judged Simpson guilty, but most blacks said he was innocent.

On the other hand...

A disabled factory worker in his 50s had been charged with raping an 8-year-old girl. His household income was about $25,000 a year and his life savings totalled $10,000. Costs for the trial came to $8,000. The man and his wife had to sell their house and move to a cheaper apartment so that he could pay his legal fees. The trial ended with a hung jury which means he

Number of lawyers in the USA, 1960–1990

(000)
800
600
400
200

1960   1970   1980   1990

Number of Lawyers in the US per 100,000 of the population
1960 – 145/100,000
1990 – 301/100,000

Figure 4.17

has to find the money for a new trial.

In most murder cases, the defendant is poor. "They may not have started that way but for anyone other than the super rich, they will be poor before the case is over," says Larry Hammond, a criminal lawyer in Phoenix, Arizona.

HEALTH CARE IN THE USA

How America pays for its health care

The USA does not have a National Health Service like Britain. In the USA people have to take out private insurance for themselves and their families or get a job where their employer will pay it for them. The main medical insurance companies are Blue Cross and Blue Shield. This accounts for about half of the money spent on health care in the USA—over $380 billion in 1991.

The other half of health care spending is government money. People over 65 get Medicare and poor people can get Medicaid. These are paid for by the government, but they do not cover all treatments and many doctors and hospitals refuse to treat people unless they have private insurance.

In 1991 the government spent $118 billion on Medicare. This provided health care for over 35 million elderly and disabled Americans. In the same year over $110 billion was spent on Medicaid. This provided much of the health care available to the poor. Over 331 million people received Medicaid in 1992. Medicaid has too few doctors and a high proportion of patients with AIDS and drug abuse problems. Nearly 30% of Medicaid money is spent on long-term care for the mentally retarded.

There are some free hospitals which collect money from churches and other charities and get some funds from the government. They treat the people that nobody else will.

The USA spends 13.3% of its GDP on health care. This is more than double what is spent in the UK and more than any other country in the world. However, this does not mean that every American is healthy. It does not mean that every American gets the same opportunity to be treated if he or she is ill. It does not seem to help them to live longer.

	Percentage of income spent on health	Life Expectancy
USA	13.3	75.6
UK	6.6	75.8
Spain	6.5	77.4
Japan	6.8	78.6

Table 4.12

Americans spent over $800 billion on health care in 1992. This has grown very quickly since 1980 when they spent $250 billion on their health.

Costs have gone up quickly because
- people live longer
- doctors are paid high salaries—there are 600,000 doctors in the USA, each earning on average $170,000 (£118,000)
- new treatments are more expensive
- doctors give treatments when they do not need to in case they are sued
- insurance companies make big profits
- insurance companies employ large numbers of workers to run the system

The effect of this on an average family is that their health insurance premiums have risen sharply over the last few years. For example, in Florida, the annual premium for a family insured through the state employee system rose from $840 in 1980 to $3,765 in 1990. In 1993, Florida spent more on its Medicaid programme than on its schools.

It will cost up to $10,000 per year for a family of 4 living in New York to get full health and dental care from Blue Cross and Blue Shield.

As the cost of insurance has risen it means that, increasingly, people or their employers cannot afford to pay the premiums. Each year the number of people who are not covered by health insurance increases. (see Figure 4.18)

Nearly 86% of Americans have health insurance, but this figure disguises another fact, namely that many are underinsured because of the high cost of the premiums for certain forms of treatment. Those most likely to be insured are the elderly, the employed and those educated to at least high school diploma level.

Finding a doctor can be a problem for Medicaid patients

Sherri Williams of Tennessee discovered that she was pregnant. Although she qualified for Medicaid, Sherri could not find a doctor who would look after her. She eventually got her first doctor's appointment when she was 7 months pregnant. Three days before that first visit, she went into labour. Her daughter, Cassandra, was born with brain damage and had to be in hospital for months. According to Cassandra's doctor, Sherri's pregnancy was "complicated by a lack of prenatal care."

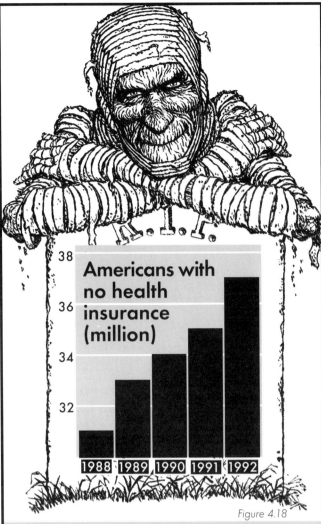

Americans with no health insurance (million)

38
36
34
32

1988 1989 1990 1991 1992

Figure 4.18

Some consequences of being uninsured

* lack of coverage for routine care which can detect and cure health problems before they become serious.

* you only get medical help when a condition is serious.

* you are up to twice as likely as an insured patient to be at risk of dying when you reach the hospital door.

* you have less access to high cost technology which might help to save your life.

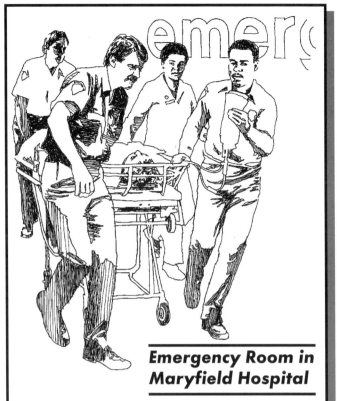

Emergency Room in Maryfield Hospital

This is where mostly uninsured and underinsured people come for emergency treatment. They do not receive general medical care on a regular basis and so have to rely on emergency room visits. Very often drug abusers or poor people who suffer from AIDS or TB are unwilling to go for regular medical care. They go to emergency rooms when they desperately need help. Doctors use the full range of medical technology to help these patients. The average cost of a visit to an emergency room is $165. Sixteen percent of people treated in Maryfield Hospital each year are charity cases. They do not pay anything. Their treatment is paid for by taxpayers and patients with private insurance.

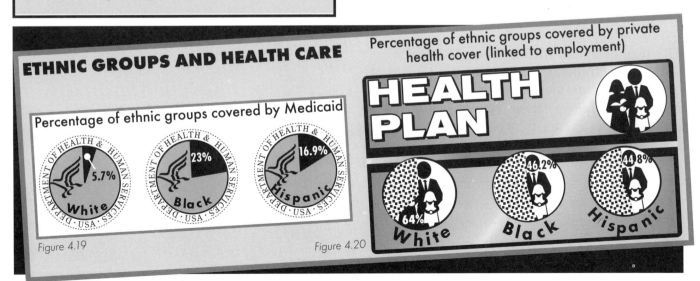

ETHNIC GROUPS AND HEALTH CARE

Percentage of ethnic groups covered by private health cover (linked to employment)

Percentage of ethnic groups covered by Medicaid

White 5.7%
Black 23%
Hispanic 16.9%

Figure 4.19

HEALTH PLAN

White 64%
Black 46.2%
Hispanic 44.8%

Figure 4.20

GREATER EQUALITY OF HEALTH CARE IN THE USA

Many politicians have argued for and promised to reform the US health system to ensure that a minimum cover is available for everyone.

> I will propose a programme to ensure that no American family will be prevented from obtaining basic medical care by inability to pay. President Richard Nixon 22 January 1971

> **Health care isn't a matter of privilege but a fundamental human right.**
> *Senator Harris Wofford 1 June 1991*

In 1993, President Clinton set up a group to look at National Health Care Reform. The group was headed by Hillary Clinton and its aim was to devise a plan for overhauling the health care system

Here are some of the suggestions made by the group

- To retain the private insurance system but force it to compete to keep costs down.

- To define a set of minimum health care standards that all insurance plans can meet.

- Doctors should carry out more preventive medicine.

- Pharmacies should supply more generic medicines instead of expensive brand names.

- Save money and reduce the federal budget.

- Government to pay for these reforms either by savings or by increasing taxes.

The proposals ran into fierce resistance from a number of groups in the US including insurance companies, doctors and large sections of the Democrat and Republican Parties. They objected because it was the state interfering in private business. It was ideologically inappropriate for the USA. The proposals were dropped and the group made no progress.

Activities

1 How do Americans pay for their health care?

2 Americans spend twice as much of their income on health as people in the UK. Does this lead to them being healthier? Justify your answer.

3 Draw a graph to illustrate the increase in health spending by Americans between 1980 and 1992.

4 Why has health spending increased so much?

5 What is the effect of this on health insurance costs in the USA?

6 What effects have increased costs had on health insurance coverage in the USA in recent years?

7 *"The lack of health insurance and inadequate insurance can be a problem for people in the USA."*

   Do you agree or disagree? Justify your answer.

8 Does membership of an ethnic group affect your access to medical care in the US? Explain your answer.

9 Why did the attempts by the Clinton Administration to alter the system fail?

10 According to the American Dream, *"all people have equal opportunities to get health care in the USA."*

   Using the information in this section decide whether this is true or not. Explain your answer using examples.

FACTFILE: US Education

There is no such thing as an American school system. Instead, there is a mixture of different state and local systems.

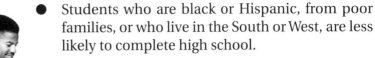

- 73% of mothers with school age children work outside the home. One school age child in four lives in a home with a single parent. Only one school child in fourteen lives in the classic home of two adults one of whom is the wage earner.

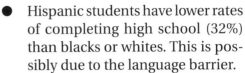

- Students who are black or Hispanic, from poor families, or who live in the South or West, are less likely to complete high school.

  - Hispanic students have lower rates of completing high school (32%) than blacks or whites. This is possibly due to the language barrier.

  - Black students' high school graduation rate rose to nearly 84% in 1993 from 74% in 1992. Among whites, the rate rose to 90% from 85%.

- Dropout rates for black pupils are soaring. Pupils are switched off by a combination of poverty and poor schooling. 78% of America's largest urban schools reported an increase in the dropout rate for black children for 1992–93. This contrasts with a reduction in the national dropout rate—even the dropout rate among inner city children of *all* ethnic groups is falling.

- More than a quarter of the girls who drop out of high school give pregnancy as their reason.

- About 8% of male dropouts say they left school because they had become fathers.

- The most common reason for dropping out is still a dislike of school.

- Inner cities are suffering a teacher shortage which is twice the national average.

- There should be more ethnic minority teachers to help to lower the dropout rate.

- More money should be spent on urban children. On average, suburbs spend $437 (£260) more on each child than the big cities.

Figure 4.21

YEARS OF COMPLETED SCHOOL (1991/92) (%)		Hispanic	Asian/Pacific Islanders	Blacks	Whites
Elementary	(0–8 years)	33.6	11.1	13.3	9.0
High school	(1–3 years)	15.1	5.2	19.1	10.1
	(4 years)	29.3	26.6	35.7	36.4
College	(1–3 years)	12.3	17.8	20.1	22.5
	(4 years+)	9.7	39.4	11.9	22.1

Table 4.13

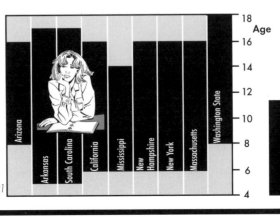

Compulsory school attendance in some states in the USA

A good education is important for anyone wishing to improve their chances of making money in the USA. (See Table 4.14) Therefore, education is a fundamental part of the American Dream—a way of 'bettering oneself' and 'rising in the world'. For this reason the millions of immigrants coming to the USA often tied their hopes for a better life to a good education for themselves and their children.

People who have...	Average Annual Income (USA 1990)
no High School diploma	$14,000
a High School Diploma	$19,000
a Degree	$32,700
a Doctorate	$53,700
a Professor's Degree	$65,600

Table 4.14

Education in the USA was believed to serve the goal of 'Americanisation'. Schools in the USA brought together the hundreds of cultural and linguistic groups, various religions and the many different social and political backgrounds represented by the millions of immigrants.

For several decades, public policy and legal decisions have given ethnic minorities certain rights in the area of education. For example, the Bilingual Education Act has meant that children whose first language is not English must be taught in their mother tongue, be it Spanish, Navaho or Cantonese. This means that about 80 languages are being used for instruction in American schools.

Thomas Corcoran High School, Syracuse, New York

An armed policeman patrols outside in the corridor.

The windowless room in the basement of Thomas Corcoran High School is known as B5. There are no wall decorations and no books on the bookshelf. Because of overcrowding, this is home 8 periods a day, 5 days a week to Option 2 class—14 male teenagers. This class has some of the country's toughest and most disadvantaged children. The teacher, Mr Pryor, says that "even with knives, they're still kids. They can be saved. They want to learn—they just don't know how." Also in the class is a security man and an armed policeman patrols outside in the corridor. Corcoran has 1,322 pupils aged 14 to 18, about 90 full-time and part-time teachers, is 50/50 white and non-white and has a dropout rate of 40%.

"In what people call the good old days, many kids didn't make it to high school at all. That was OK. There were jobs then but there aren't now."

Case study 1

Thomas Jefferson High School for Science and Technology

Case study 2

Jefferson is one of the best schools in the USA. This is proved by the fact that they did better in 1990 and 1991 than any other school in the national 'scholastic aptitude test.'

The school is situated in the wealthy middle-class suburbs of northern Virginia. There are 1,660 students and 120 teachers. Many of these students do not go to their local school, but may travel as much as 60 miles to get to Jefferson. It is a 'magnet' school. It has its own higher-than-average entrance standards. Of the 2,000 applicants annually, only 400 make the grade. The school specialises in Maths, technology and the sciences. Much of the sophisticated equipment is donated by businesses.

Seventy four percent of its students are white and twenty one percent are of Asian origin. Only five percent are black. It is 60% male and 40% female. Its dropout rate is virtually nonexistent.

Percentage of students remaining at school and college by ethnic background			
Age	White	Black	Hispanic
16–17	93	92	83
18–19	60	56	48
20–21	43	30	26

Table 4.15

Lack of education can lead to unemployment.

✎ In 1991, 11% of the population who dropped out of High School before completing 4 years were unemployed.

✎ 14.7% of blacks who did not complete 4 years of High School were unemployed.

✎ Of the people who completed more than 4 years of High School, only 2.8% were unemployed.

✎ More blacks and Hispanics drop out of High School and are, therefore, more likely to be unemployed.

✎ In the '50s and '60s, people who dropped out of school or who did badly at school could find well-paid, unskilled jobs in local factories. However, many of these jobs shifted abroad where labour is cheaper. So today lack of education often means unemployment or low-paid jobs, while a better education leads to a higher income.

✎ In the ghetto the only well-paid job opportunities for most school dropouts is dealing in drugs. Hence the attraction of drug dealing and the violence used by gangs to protect their territory.

Activities

1 **"The better your education the higher your standard of living."**

Do you agree or disagree with this statement? Justify your answer.

2 How have the American education authorities tried to provide equal access to education for the ethnic minority groups in the USA?

3 Do ethnic minority groups have equality in education in the USA? Explain your answer.

4 What effect does education have on the employment prospects of blacks and Hispanics?

5 **"Education is a fundamental part of the American Dream—a way of 'bettering oneself' and 'rising in the world'."**

To what extent does education in the USA today meet this view of the American Dream? Justify your answer.

HOUSING AND HOMELESSNESS

A 1988 estimate suggested that there were at least 600,000 homeless people in the US. A government study in 1994 stated that there were as many as 7 million people made homeless temporarily between 1985 and 1990.

Homelessness grew throughout the 1980s for a variety of reasons.

⬠ Mental institutions were closed and patients were sent into the community which could not meet their needs. Many ended up without homes.

⬠ Easy supply of drugs meant that the addiction rate rose and many drug addicts ended up on the streets.

⬠ Many inner city ghettos were developed into shopping centres, expensive offices and houses. A lack of cheap housing meant that more people ended up homeless.

⬠ Unemployment and poverty can also lead to homelessness.

In 1985 the homeless were mainly single men. By 1995 half of the homeless population were families with children.

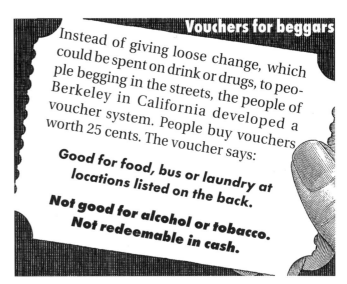

Vouchers for beggars

Instead of giving loose change, which could be spent on drink or drugs, to people begging in the streets, the people of Berkeley in California developed a voucher system. People buy vouchers worth 25 cents. The voucher says:

Good for food, bus or laundry at locations listed on the back.

Not good for alcohol or tobacco. Not redeemable in cash.

People buy books of vouchers for $2 or $5. The experiment involves 27 stores which sell vouchers and 15 outlets that accept them. The Berkeley Emergency Food Project, which offers dinners for 25 cents, reports that there has been an increase in the number of people eating its dinners. Other cities have been watching the experiment with interest.

FACTFILE: US Housing

Inner City Ghetto

- housing is run-down with poorly lit streets, few local shops and no doctors
- plumbing and sanitation do not work
- streets are not cleaned and refuse is not collected regularly; rats and cockroaches are common
- play parks are vandalised and children play in the street
- drunks and junkies lie in hallways and on landings
- landlords often burn down houses to collect the insurance
- tenants often burn down the houses to be rehoused in better places

Inner City Apartments

- apartments have doormen to control who gets in
- security cameras in corridors and on stairs
- emergency security buttons connected to doorman and police
- only very rich businessmen, politicians, doctors, lawyers or entertainers can afford to live there
- apartments cleaned by maids and the block is kept clean by janitors
- may have a swimming pool, sun lounge, fitness suite and even a garden on the roof

High Class Suburbs

- mainly white
- estate surrounded by walls and fences which are often electrified and have sensors to warn of intruders
- guardhouse on road. Entry by invitation only.
- guests must drive to their host's house without stopping
- video cameras concealed in the trees
- undersoil sensors to detect trespassers
- each home has a wall or fence
- each house has security lights
- houses have guard dogs
- people do not walk in the common spaces between the houses

Middle-class Black or White Suburbs

- large detached houses with well-tended lawns
- tree-lined streets, well-lit at night
- houses with security lights
- streets patrolled regularly by police
- youths not allowed to gather after dusk
- parents drive children everywhere, or as they grow older they have their own cars
- separate suburbs for whites and blacks. Although segregation is not allowed, people 'know' where they they would not be wanted.
- good schools with modern equipment and the best teachers

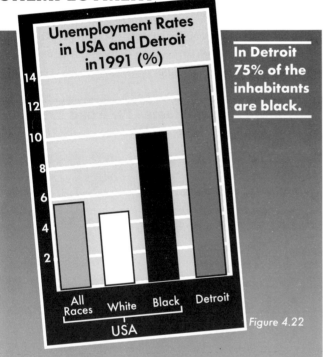

Activities

1 Read the checklists on the different types of housing in a US city.

Write a description of what life is like in each of these areas.

Highlight any advantages or disadvantages that people will have if they live in these areas.

2 How large is the problem of homelessness in the US? Give figures to support your answer.

3 What are the major causes of homelessness?

4 Why would people prefer to give vouchers to homeless beggars rather than cash?

UNEMPLOYMENT

Unemployment Rates in USA and Detroit in 1991 (%)

In Detroit 75% of the inhabitants are black.

All Races / White / Black — USA
Detroit

Figure 4.22

Unemployment means that all Americans are not equal. Unemployment can lead to

● low standards of living (poverty)
● low self-respect
● crime
● poor housing or homelessness
● poor health
● poor education

Unemployment is not shared equally amongst ethnic groups and it is a major problem in many American cities. From Figure 4.22 we can see that unemployment in Detroit is 13.8%—far higher than the average unemployment rate for the USA as a whole. Unemployment is also a problem in areas of rural America.

POVERTY — AN AMERICAN REALITY

The American Dream leads us to believe that all Americans are rich and have a high standard of living. The reality is that there are millions of poor people in the US. All Americans are not equal.

In 1991, nearly 36 million Americans were described by the government as poor. Many cannot afford the basic necessities. Some do not have homes. Many live in homes that are substandard. Many cannot afford medical care. Many turn to drugs, guns and crime to get money.

Between 1973 and 1988 the poor got poorer. The income of the poorest people in the US fell by 9%, so the poor were able to buy even less. Poverty is worst among blacks and Hispanics. One white person in 10 is poor, while 1 out of every 3 black people is poor and 1 out of every 4 Hispanics is poor.

Children suffer more from poverty than any other single group in the USA. While 14% of all Americans are poor, this rises to 21% for children who live in a poor family. Forty five percent of black children live in a poor family.

A child who lives in a poor family will not get the same opportunity of education or health as the child of a rich family.

Activities

1 **"Unemployment means that all Americans are not equal."**

Do you agree or disagree with this statement? Explain your answer.

2 Draw a spider diagram to show what unemployment can lead to.

3 **"Unemployment is not shared equally by all ethnic groups and it is a major problem in many American cities."**

To what extent is this true?

4 What is meant by poverty?

5 Describe the level of poverty in the US and what has happened to poor people over recent years.

6 Which groups suffer most from poverty in the USA?

7 **"The American Dream leads us to believe that all Americans are rich and have a high standard of living."**

Do you agree or disagree with this statement? Explain your answer.

AFFIRMATIVE ACTION

Affirmative action was an attempt to increase the employment opportunities for women and ethnic minorities and so overcome the past patterns of discrimination in the USA.

Under the Equal Opportunity Act (1972) all companies doing work for the Federal government, state governments, local governments and institutions like universities had to plan to increase the proportion of female and ethnic minority employees and students until they were equal to the proportion of these groups in the community. However, a number of Supreme Court cases ruled that affirmative action plans which laid down racial quotas were unconstitutional. As a result, many affirmative action programmes are being dismantled.

In 1995, the University of California voted to end twenty years of affirmative action in admission and hiring because in "fundamental fairness" the University should not "trample individual rights" to give preference to group rights. For twenty years up to 40% of University of California students have been admitted for reasons other than academic merit.

The decision caused much controversy including a demonstration led by the Rev. Jesse Jackson, but the University of California has gone ahead with its decision. The new colour-blind admission system seems set to alter the ethnic composition of the university—mainly to the benefit of Asian American students.

University of California — admissions by ethnic group (%)		
	1995 with affimative action	**1997** (projected)
Blacks	4.0	2.0
Hispanics	13.0	11.0
Asian Americans	30.0	40.0+
Whites	50.0+	50.0-

Table 4.16

California is now gearing up for another initiative in 1996—the California Civil Rights Initiative (CCRI). Supporters need 650,000 signatures to get the Initiative on the ballot paper. That is expected to be easy. Its main provision is a restatement of the 1964 Civil Rights Act. The State of California or its agents will not use "race, sex, colour, ethnicity or national origin as a criterion for either discriminating against or granting preferential treatment to any individual

or groups ..." Effectively this initiative would put an end to over 20 years of preferential programmes aimed at the minorities.

HOW EFFECTIVE HAS AFFIRMATIVE ACTION BEEN?

Affirmative Action has been of some benefit for women and the ethnic minorities. They have now gained access to, and promotion in, many areas of employment where previously they had been excluded.

Affirmative Action has led to a growing number of women in posts of seniority in government institutions and private business in the US.

Women have made important progress in obtaining jobs in managerial and professional occupations. In 1983 they held 40% of these high paying jobs, a figure which rose to 48% in 1993. Despite this, women are still over-represented in low paid jobs and, on average, women still only earn about 77% of average male earnings.

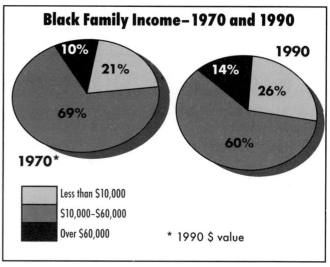

Figure 4.23

Affirmative Action has also led to the growth of a black middle class. In the 1970s and 1980s the black middle class expanded rapidly. One-third of American blacks are now middle class. They have moved to the suburbs, looking for better schools, safer streets and better services.

Nevertheless, at the same time the number of blacks earning less than $10,000 increased from 21% to 26%. Affirmative action and equal opportunities has not given them any advantage. The suburbs are segregated. Middle-class blacks overwhelmingly live in black suburbs. Studies show that whites are happy to live beside blacks as long as the proportion of blacks does not exceed 8%. Over that figure whites begin to move out, property values begin to fall and the area rapidly becomes all black. Estate agents steer blacks away from white areas and banks are more reluctant to lend to blacks than they are to whites.

Some whites resent affirmative action programmes because of the dangers of reverse discrimination. Increasingly, liberal white America is turning away from such programmes partly due to their cost in an era of economic problems, and partly because many think that the ethnic minorities should stop waiting for handouts and should begin to take action themselves to improve their lifestyles.

Busing

Busing was introduced in the early 1970s in an attempt to achieve racial balance in schools. Children from predominantly white areas were taken by bus across cities to schools in black areas and black children were bused to schools in white areas. This policy led to great opposition from both black and white communities in various US cities.

By the 1990s, busing students in order to desegregate schools in US cities had ceased to be an important programme. It was allowed to wither as the result of major opposition to it from parents and students in all communities. Educationalists began to suggest that black children achieved more in all-black schools. White flight had taken too many white students out of the cities to make busing realistic

and the Reagan and Bush Administrations were not very friendly towards the programme.

How do blacks and whites compare? (Figures for 1990s)	Whites	Blacks
Percentage of total US population	74.2	12.5
Percentage of prison population	39.6	46.3
Children whose mothers never married (%)	2.7	35.3
Children living only with mothers (%)	14.2	51.2
Life expectancy (Years)	76.0	70.3
Infant mortality rates(per 100 births)	8.1	16.5
Believed OJ Simpson was guilty (%)	57.5	17.5

Table 4.17

Activities

1 What were the aims of Affirmative Action?

2 What has Affirmative Action achieved over 20 years?

3 What was busing and why has it ceased to be relevant in the 1990s?

4 Using the statistics in table 4.17 write a report comparing blacks and whites.

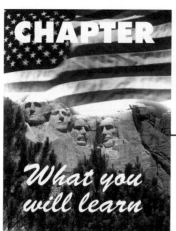

CHAPTER 4

What you will learn

THE USA – SECTION 6

IS THE MOSAIC FRACTURING?

1   There may be less cooperation and support than in the past between ethnic groups in the USA .

2   There are extremists in the USA who want the ethnic groups to be less cooperative.

Sonny Carson, a self-styled urban guerrilla who leads a group called the X-Clan, claimed that "There is a white plot to destroy the blacks of America. The conspiracy is widespread."

If such beliefs are widely held, it is increasingly likely that the mosaic is about to fracture in the 1990s.

LOS ANGELES SOUTH CENTRAL — A RIOT WAITING TO HAPPEN

Between 1970 and 1990 the population of Los Angeles grew by 20%, but it became more fragmented and dispersed. High tech industry developed on the periphery and much of it was financed by defence contracts. With the end of the Cold War, many of these contracts dried up and Los Angeles faced eco-nomic problems which made it less inclined to help its more unfortunate inhabitants.

Under Reagan and Bush, spending on anti-poverty programmes was slashed. Subsidised housing expenditure fell by 82%, job training and employment aid was cut by 63% and community service and development programmes were reduced by 40%.

Inner city LA has a fragmented population of 1.7 million Hispanics, 800,000 African Americans, 600,000 Jews and sizeable communities of Chinese, Koreans, Filipinos and people from central America. These people jostle with each other in a low wage, high unemployment economy. This creates tensions which can lead to racial distrust, envy and hatred. These groups live close to the American Dream in the exclusive suburbs of Hollywood and Bel Air. They see it but they cannot have it which leads to frustration.

Living standards in South Central, an area of LA, are on a par with those found in the Third World. Children grow up in poor housing conditions, often five or more to a room. They do not know who their fathers are and their mothers are often crack addicts or alcoholics. Men hang out in illegal drinking dens or take drugs. Apart from drink and drugs there is hardly any other form of entertainment in the area. There is just one cinema in South Central.

The high school dropout rate is over 50% and more than 30% of those who attend school regularly truant. Armed guards stand at the door of every classroom to protect the teachers from the pupils and the police patrol the playgrounds.

Many residents do not feel that they are part of society any more.

LA Riots 1992

On 3 March 1991 video pictures of the arrest and beating of Rodney King shocked America and the world. While 25 police officers stood around, King—

Los Angeles, the scene of riots in 1992 after a court freed four white policemen accused of attacking a black man.

Washington, the capital of the USA has one of the highest murder rates in the country.

a black motorist stopped for speeding and being drunk—was shot twice by a stun gun, kicked repeatedly and bludgeoned 56 times. Four white police officers were tried for the crime. They were found innocent in April 1992 and this lead to the Los Angeles Riots.

The riot left 53 people dead and 1,400 homes and businesses were burned and looted. The majority of the businesses belonged to Koreans who owned shops and small-scale factories in the area. Their success at making money in these ghetto areas made them a target for resentment from poor unemployed black residents of South Central LA.

This was one of the worst riots in US history. It lasted for 5 nights and spread to more affluent adjoining areas. Both black and Hispanic gang members were involved in the looting. However, while it spread to the more affluent white areas it did not affect the neighbouring Hispanic barrio. Looters drove to suburban shopping malls in search of luxury goods which were unavailable locally.

It took the police and the army several days to regain limited control of the streets. The mayor imposed a dusk to dawn curfew and the police needed the help of 1,000 federal police, and 6,000 National Guards. Four thousand US Marines were placed on standby. Although more than 2,000 looters were arrested, only 65 people have been charged with arson and only 5 suspected of murder.

There was a great deal of political activity after the riots, discussing and promising economic and social help for rebuilding and repairing the destruction. Money was promised but very little was delivered. The area still lives on its two main sources of income—from welfare and drugs.

NEW YORK 1991

Racial violence flared in New York after a Hasidic Jew killed a black child in a motor accident. In the riot which followed, a 22-year-old Jewish student was stabbed to death and many police officers were injured when they were attacked by bricks, bottles and shotguns as they tried to regain control. Groups of black youths roamed the streets shouting 'Heil Hitler' and threw bricks through the windows of Jewish homes. They threatened to drive the Jews from the area. Even David Dinkins, the first black Mayor of New York, was showered by bottles and abuse when he went to try to help restore order. Although the majority of the rioters were native black Americans, they were joined by a large number of young West Indian immigrants.

WASHINGTON DC RIOTS 1991

In May 1991 the police used teargas and imposed a curfew between midnight and 5am in a Hispanic district less than two miles from the White House after a second night of rioting in the capital. The riot was sparked off by the shooting of a Hispanic man while being arrested by police. Several hundred youths, armed with stones and petrol bombs, fought running battles with police, looted shops and set fire to cars and buildings. The Hispanic community complained that the reason for the riot was an alleged history of harassment from the mainly black police force as well as high unemployment, overcrowded housing, poor education and an administration which they claimed ignored their needs.

The administration of Washington is dominated by black representatives as the capital has a 70% black population. The Hispanic population is only 10% and does not have political influence. The language barrier is one of the reasons which prevents participation in the political process. Therefore Hispanics are under-represented. Less than 3% of police officers in Washington are Hispanic.

THE MILLION MAN MARCH

"The headlines of murder and mayhem have created ugly images of black men as thieves, criminals and savages. We have deemed it necessary to call for one million disciplined, committed and dedicated black men, from all walks of life in America, to march on Washington, showing the world a vastly different picture of the black male."
(march organiser)

Louis Farrakhan is leader of the *Nation of Islam,* an Islamic group which has been accused of preaching separatism and racism. He called for one million black American men to march on Washington on 16 October 1995. The aim of the march was to show black self-reliance. The organisers wanted black men to express their solidarity and their determination to improve their own lives and to admit that there was a great deal wrong with the way many of them have lived in the past.

The march was also a response to the deteriorating conditions faced by black people in general and black men in particular. Black people are faced with a Republican Party, and increasing public opinion, that wants tough restrictions on social spending, particularly welfare, and the ending of Affirmative Action. The failure of Civil Rights and Affirmative Action to secure equality and the economic cost of these programmes is leading to disharmony in the USA. The Civil Rights aim of racial integration is being replaced by calls for separatism.

Farrakhan and his followers make extreme statements against Jews and Catholics and claim that AIDS and drugs are plagues engineered by whites to decimate the black race.

The Nation of Islam runs effective programmes against drugs and crime in depressed inner city areas and has over 30,000 followers. Farrakhan has become increasingly influential particularly among black students because civil rights leaders have failed to show effective leadership. He advocates racial separation.

Some analysts consider the success of the march illustrates a significant power shift in the black community away from the integrationist policies of the old civil rights movement towards the more aggressive separatist stance of Farrakhan and the Nation of Islam. The vast majority of those on the march rejected Farrakhan's anti-Semitism and his contempt for white people, women and homosexuals. Most were there to reassert themselves and create a positive image of the black male. They were not there to separate themselves from other ethnic groups in the USA.

THE OKLAHOMA BOMBING

On 19 April 1995 the Alfred Murrah Federal Building in Oklahoma City was blown up by a huge bomb. In the worst peacetime attack on American soil, 168 people were killed and over 400 injured. Destruction was estimated at $330 million with 199 buildings damaged or destroyed. The blast, which was felt 30 miles away, left a crater eight feet deep by thirty feet wide in the street.

Originally American politicians and the public suspected and accused Arab-Muslim extremists. They were horrified when extreme right-wing, anti-government Americans were arrested for planting the bomb. Twenty seven-year-old Gulf War veteran Timothy McVeigh was charged but strong suspicion existed that several others were involved—all with links to patriotic militia groups.

Investigators found documents relating to events at Waco in McVeigh's car. In 1993, the FBI and the ATF (Bureau of Alcohol, Tobacco and Firearms) had laid siege to the Branch Davidian Compound in Waco,

200 miles south of Oklahoma, after the heavily armed occupants had opened fire on them. The Oklahoma bomb was exactly two years to the day after the FBI and the ATF had stormed the compound and 86 men, women and children had been killed. Among the offices in the Federal building in Oklahoma City were those belonging to the FBI and the ATF.

McVeigh had publicly threatened revenge and press reports claimed he had made a pilgrimage to Waco to view the charred remains. However, in 1996 there was still confusion regarding who was responsible.

THE IMPACT OF THE BOMBING

After the Oklahoma bombing President Clinton approved plans to implement anti-terrorist measures within the USA. New powers were given to the FBI to infiltrate any organisation that proposed illegal (anti-government) violence, to tap telephones and to check the personal records of anyone suspected of terrorist involvement. However, such measures may clash with the civil liberties built into the American Bill of Rights.

There is increasing evidence that the views of the 'Patriots' are attracting wider support than is generally believed. Tee-shirts with such slogans as "I love my country but I fear my government" are becoming more common. Media broadcasts which champion the rights of the individual against the state and federal authorities are attracting larger audiences. Local militias have sprouted in many of the states across the country. There is no national structure for these groups but there does exist a common dislike of federal government personnel and policies which is often passed on via computer billboards and Internet facilities.

The remains of the Alfred Murrah Federal Building in Oklahoma City were eventually demolished.

Activities

1 Explain in your own words why the Oklahoma bombing occurred.

2 Why is the Oklahoma bombing an important event in the USA?

3 ***"Is the Mosaic fracturing?"***

What is meant by this statement? Using the information available, do you think it is true?

1   What is meant by Communism.

2   How Communism was applied under the leadership of Mao.

3   How the interpretation of Communism has changed under the leadership of Deng.

WHAT IS COMMUNISM?

Communism is the political ideology which dominates life in China. In the early 1990s China was the only major country left in the world which was run under the Communist system. The Communist leaderships in the Soviet Union and Eastern Europe were swept away during a period of rapid change in the late 1980s.

The ideas behind Communism were developed by Karl Marx, a German philosopher who lived in the nineteenth century. He believed that everyone belonged to one of two classes. People were either part of the *Bourgeoisie*, who owned factories and businesses, or the *Proletariat*, who worked as labourers for the owning class. Marx believed that the Proletariat would eventually realise that the Bourgeoisie were taking advantage of them, and that they would rise up in revolution. After the revolution the wealth would be evenly distributed among all the people, and there would be no class distinction.

Marx believed that his revolution would take place in either Britain or Germany. However, it was in Russia in the early years of the twentieth century that his philosophy was put into practice. Lenin led a Communist revolution in Russia, and began to run the country under a system of Communism called Marxism-Leninism.

Communism aimed to take the vast wealth from the Bourgeoisie and distribute it evenly amongst the Proletariat. It aimed to end all distinctions between the classes and the sexes. Revolutionary leaders in China followed the example from neighbouring Russia and established a Communist government in 1949.

Karl Marx would have described Communism as an economic theory, aimed at achieving an equal distribution of wealth amongst everyone. In China Communism has become an ideology which domi-

nates the political and social life of the country as well as the economy.

THE CHINESE SYSTEM OF COMMUNISM UNDER MAO

The Communist Revolution in China was led by Mao Zedong, who led the country from 1949 until his death in 1976. He was inspired by the ideas of Karl Marx, and by the changes which he saw in Russia following the successful revolution there.

Conditions were terrible in China in the first half of the twentieth century. The country was run by a tiny privileged group, and ordinary people lived a peasant lifestyle, often having to put up with dreadful hardships. In the 1920s and '30s the Kuomintang (People's Party) was the main opposition voice, but after a disagreement, Mao Zedong broke away from it to form the Communist Party of China.

The Communists and the Kuomintang fought a Civil War in the late 1940s which ended in victory for Mao Zedong and his followers, who proclaimed The People's Republic of China in 1949.

China is a one-party state. Since the revolution the Communist Party has been the only legal political voice in the country. From 1949 onwards the Communists set about transforming China into what they would describe as a 'Socialist Paradise'.

The Communist Party dominates every level of government and administration. Every key post is filled by Communist Party members, and they decide who should get all other jobs. Although in theory the government and the Communist Party are different organisations, in practice they are one and the same. Over the years the Communists have gradually removed all opposition to their policies. Mao Zedong was responsible for various purges of people who showed any signs of disagreeing with his policies. In the 1950s and 1960s opponents and critics of the

MAO ZEDONG (1893 – 1976)

Born in Shaoshan, Hunan province, son of a farmer. Mao co-founded the Chinese Communist Party in 1921. Victory in the Civil War against the Nationalists left Mao as leader of China in 1949. During the 1950s he abandoned the Soviet model of Communism and began to introduce his own ideas and reforms. His thoughts were included in his *Little Red Book*.

The Cultural Revolution

"Starting in June 1966 the *People's Daily* showered the country with one editorial after another, calling for 'establishing Chairman Mao's absolute authority', 'sweeping away all the class enemies', and encouraging people to follow Mao and join the vast undertaking of a Cultural Revolution.

In my school teaching stopped completely. All we did was study the *People's Daily* newspaper, which often devoted its whole front page to a picture of Chairman Mao. There was a daily column of Mao's sayings. I still remember the slogans in bold type, which, through reading in class over and over again, were engraved into the deepest folds of my brain: 'Chairman Mao is the red sun in our hearts!', 'Mao Zedong thought is our lifeline!', 'We will smash whoever opposes Chairman Mao!', 'People all over the world love our Great Leader Chairman Mao!'

The daily newspaper reading soon gave way to reciting and memorising The Quotations of Chairman Mao, which were collected together in a pocket sized book with a red plastic cover, known as *The Little Red Book*. Everyone was given a copy and told to cherish it 'like our eyes'.

One day we read in the *People's Daily* that an old peasant had covered the walls of his house with portraits of Chairman Mao so that he could see his face whenever he opened his eyes. We thought this was a good idea and did the same to the walls of our classroom. However, word circulated that the peasant had really used the pictures as wallpaper because they were printed on the best quality paper and were free. Rumour had it that the reporter who wrote the story had been denounced as a class enemy for encouraging 'abuse of Chairman Mao'. For the first time fear of Chairman Mao entered my consciousness…"

Adapted from *Wild Swans*, by Jung Chang, Harper Collins, London, 1991

system simply vanished into prisons or forced labour camps. Often the people who disappeared included some who had been former officials of the Communist Party or high-ranking military officers.

Mao Zedong was not willing to accept criticism of his government and its policies. He was totally convinced that his way of running China was the best, and that criticism amounted to 'counter-revolution'. Under his leadership the Communist Party played a dominant role in every aspect of people's lives. It controlled their friendships, leisure activities and even the number of children they had!

By the time of his death in 1976 Mao had become a 'God' in the eyes of the Chinese people. In fact they were probably very frightened of what the future might hold because Mao had been such a dominant influence on their lives.

THE CHINESE ECONOMY

China is a vast country in every respect. With a population of over 1,000 million it makes up almost one-quarter of the world's people. In terms of land area, China is one of the largest countries in the world, with valuable mineral deposits and natural resources. China's size and position mean that it includes many different natural regions. These range from the highest mountains in the world in the Himalayas, to the deserts of the north west, and vast plains in the east. The climate ranges from the sub-tropical to the semi-Arctic.

Given that the country is so big and so diverse, it is understandable that China has great economic potential. However, it is only since the early 1980s that China has really started to exploit this potential, and the Chinese still have a long way to go to catch up with the other major economic powers.

Before Mao Zedong's death in 1976 the Chinese economy was in a poor state. Mao did not encourage trade with other countries, and concentrated on peasant agriculture within China itself. The result of this was that living standards were very poor and the economy was outdated.

Under the Communist ideology all industries and businesses were owned by the state. The very idea of private enterprise was frowned upon. This meant that people had little incentive to work hard, and they had virtually no choice of what they could buy in shops and markets. No goods were available from outside China, and the quality of home-based products was very poor.

In the 1960s Mao developed the idea of a Cultural Revolution which involved a return to what he saw as the true ideals of Communism. This meant that he wanted to rid China of all capitalist influences. Anyone who tried to develop progressive ideas was called a 'capitalist roader' and was severely punished.

Activities

1   *"Marx believed that the Proletariat would eventually realise they were being taken advantage of by the Bourgeoisie, and that they would rise up in revolution."*

   (a) Who were the Proletariat and who were the Bourgeoisie?

   (b) In what way were the Proletariat being taken advantage of?

2   Describe the conditions in China which would have made the ideas of Communism popular.

3   What methods did Mao Zedong use to keep a tight grip on power in China?

4   What was the 'Cultural Revolution'?

5   What evidence is there in the extract from *Wild Swans* that people regarded Mao as more than just a simple political leader?

6   Summarise the main successes and failures of Mao's period as China's leader.

7   Do you think that China has changed much since then? Give evidence to support your answer.

MAO'S CHINA
The Balance of Evidence

✔ Mao gave China back its pride by making it self-reliant and self-sufficient.

✔ The commune system was developed in the countryside whereby Chinese peasants worked together to feed, clothe and provide for themselves.

✔ An egalitarian system was created which ensured equality for all. The slogan was "Serve the people".

✔ The state provided basic welfare cover for all. Education and health services were provided free for all Chinese.

✔ A low inflation rate and low crime rate were achieved.

✔ China's military strength developed and they produced their own nuclear weapons.

✗ The Great Leap Forward in the 1950s, when China was to become a great industrial nation, failed.

✗ The commune system was inefficient and gave too much power to Party officials. There was no incentive for the Chinese citizens and peasants to work hard.

✗ The Cultural Revolution created a climate of fear and economic production suffered. An estimated one million people died during the Cultural Revolution.

✗ "Red Before Expert"
The emphasis on being a 'good communist' hindered economic progress. Scientists, teachers and other skilled people were sent to the countryside to work in the fields which held back China's development.

DENG XIAOPING'S CHINA

When Mao died in 1976 he had no immediate successor. However, after a few years it was Deng who emerged as the most powerful political leader in the country. Deng was another leader of the 1949 revolution, but he had always had some reservations about Mao's policies. His official view, explained in the 1980s, was that "Mao was a Great Leader who made some mistakes". This is an obvious reference to the Cultural Revolution, when Deng himself was denounced as being a capitalist.

Under Deng there have been many changes to life in China. Politically the country remains a one-party, totalitarian state. No opposition is allowed, and when students demonstrated against the government in the late 1980s Deng cracked down hard on them. He ordered troops to open fire on unarmed protesters in Beijing's Tiananmen Square in the summer of 1989. Many of the demonstrators were killed and the leaders of the opposition were imprisoned (see pages 122–3).

However, in economic terms China has undergone major changes. In April 1993 the National People's Congress officially approved the 'Socialist Market Economy'. Chinese economists describe this as an economy in which "the market mechanism is in a key position to distribute all social resources, and government control is reduced to an overall guiding hand on the economy".

This change of policy in the 1990s has allowed free enterprise to flourish in China. People have been encouraged to start their own businesses and to produce things for their own personal profit. Foreign companies have been allowed to move into China. They see China as a huge market for their products, and also as a place where they can set up factories with low wage costs.

The result has been to improve living standards greatly for many Chinese. However, not all Chinese have benefited from Deng's economic policies, and consequently there are now great differences between rich and poor in the new China.

In Deng's China there are still many political prisoners. The leaders of the 1989 student demonstrations in Tiananmen Square were arrested and imprisoned—yet all they were campaigning for were the sort of basic human rights which people in Scotland would take for granted. Deng's China has made little progress towards granting basic rights to the people.

DENG XIAOPING

Born in Szechuan province, Deng was the son of wealthy parents, and he travelled and studied in Europe before returning to China and joining the Communist Party in 1926. He was denounced as a capitalist during the Cultural Revolution, but after the death of Mao he emerged as the new leader of China. Under his leadership, China made radical changes to its ideology and economic system.

China's economy has changed greatly under Deng. The old-fashioned Communist ideology has been changed and replaced with a more capitalist system. People are encouraged to run their own businesses and to enjoy the profits of their work. The government now describes the ideology of China as 'socialism with Chinese characteristics'.

"TO GET RICH IS GLORIOUS"

During 1992 Deng made a tour of the coastal cities which were the centre of many of his economic reforms. In a widely reported speech, he used the phrase "to get rich is glorious", once again giving his blessing to the free enterprise system which had emerged.

Deng and his government have produced a system where market forces mix with socialism. The aim is to make it possible for individuals to increase their wealth, but to maintain state control over the main centres of production. In this way, the government can still keep some control over how the wealth is distributed amongst the people.

1

FACTFILE : China

TIME CHART — MAJOR EVENTS

1934 Civil War between the Communists and the Nationalist Government led by Chiang Kai-Shek. Mao and his forces forced to escape to the mountains in the famous Long March.

1937 Japanese invasion of China.

1945 War with Japan ended.

1945–49 Civil War reopened with victory to the Communists. On 1 October 1949 Mao proclaimed the establishment of the People's Republic of China.

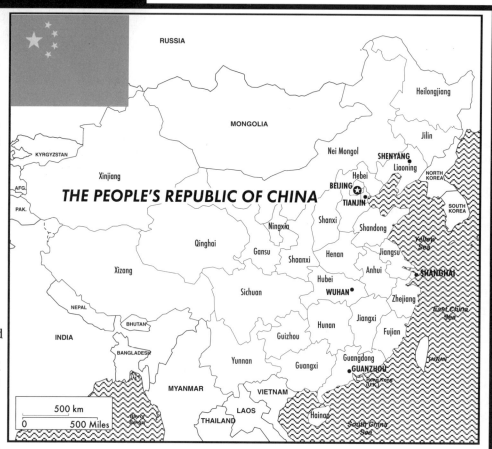

THE PEOPLE'S REPUBLIC OF CHINA

1958–60 Great Leap Forward, whereby rapid growth in both industrial and agricultural production was introduced at the same time. A disaster for China with famine occurring.

1966–69 Cultural Revolution introduced. Mao, discredited by the Great Leap Forward, made his political comeback and destroyed the moderates within the Party.

1976 Mao died and a new power struggle broke out. His widow, Madame Mao, and her associates 'The Gang of Four' were arrested and a caretaker leader Chairman Hua was appointed.

1978 Deng became the effective leader of China and introduced the Four Modernisations.

1989 June 1989 the students' protest in Tiananmen Square was crushed.

1989–95 Deng remained as 'paramount leader'. Jiang Zemin became Party Leader and hard-liner Le Peng remained as Premier.

Area	9,571,300 km²
Population	1,133,682,501 (approximately 20 times the population of Britain, 4 times the population of the USA)
Capital City	Beijing (Population 11 million)
Other Main Cities	Shanghai (14 million), Tianjin (9 million), Shenyang (5 million), Wuhan (4 million), Guangzhou (4 million).
Highest Mountain	Mount Everest (8,848 metres)
Longest River	Yangtse (5,470 kilometres)
Official Language	Mandarin Chinese
Major Religions	Buddhism, Daoism, Confucianism, Islam, Christianity
Money	1 Yuan = 10 Jiao = 100 Fen
Economy	The countryside is dominated by agriculture. Cities are becoming more industrial.
Major Resources	Coal, iron ore, oil, natural gas, tin etc. China's great rivers can be used to generate electricity.
Major Products	Main agricultural products are wheat, tea, rice and soya beans. Industrial products include paper, textiles and manufactures for foreign companies.

In Deng Xiaoping's China capitalism has been allowed to develop under government control.

SOCIALISM WITH CHINESE CHARACTERISTICS

Article 1 of the
Constitution of the People's Republic of China

"The People's Republic of China is a socialist state under the people's democratic dictatorship led by the working class and based on the alliance of workers and peasants.

The socialist system is the basic system of the People's Republic of China. Disruption of the socialist system by any organisation or individual is prohibited."

Activities

1 Summarise the main changes which Deng has made to the Chinese economy.

2 What is meant by the phrase "socialism with Chinese characteristics"?

3 In your opinion, is it true to say that China is a major world superpower? Give reasons for your answer.

You should consider factors such as:
- Wealth and Economic Power
- International Influence
- Military Power
- Population

4

SOURCE 1 Features of Communist Theory

- ✪ All industries and businesses owned by the government
- ✪ All people have equal incomes
- ✪ Society is run in the best interests of all people
- ✪ Communist Party to dominate all aspects of life

SOURCE 2 Features of Life in China in the 1990s

- ✪ Huge divide between the rich and the poor
- ✪ 75% of output now comes from private businesses
- ✪ Crime, violence and drug abuse rising
- ✪ Communist Party outlaws all opposition groups

"China is a good example of how Communist Theory can work."
View of a Chinese Politician

Using evidence from the sources above, say if you agree with the view expressed by the Chinese politician.

CHAPTER 5

CHINA – SECTION 2
THE CHANGING CHINESE ECONOMY

What you will learn

1 The nature of the changes in the Chinese economy since the late 1970s: *The Four Modernisations; The Great Leap Outwards; The Open Door Policy.*

2 Problems associated with the economic changes.

THE CHINESE ECONOMY

Under Deng Xiaoping's leadership, the Chinese economy has made great advances. In the late 1970s a major programme of economic reform and modernisation was introduced. The Chinese tend to give such programmes grand titles. This one was called 'The Four Modernisations'.

The government believed it was essential to modernise the Chinese economy in four key areas—agriculture, industry, science/technology and defence. All of these areas had been held back during Mao's rule. To encourage the Four Modernisations, Deng also tried to develop links between China and other countries, ending the long period of isolation. The new leadership realised that if the Four Modernisations were to succeed, China would need help from countries which already had experience of modern technology. For this reason China went to countries such as the UK, the USA and France. This policy was known as 'The Great Leap Outwards', echoing 'The Great Leap Forward' which had been the industrial plan in the late 1950s.

THE FOUR MODERNISATIONS

China's main agricultural products are grain (including rice), tea and cotton. The methods used to produce them were inefficient, concentrating on large numbers of workers. Although this meant that everyone in the country could be employed, one of the features of the Four Modernisations was a switch to greater mechanisation. Agricultural methods were also improved with better drainage and irrigation systems, and the use of modern fertilisers and pesticides. The result was to increase agricultural output and improve the reliability and quantity of food supplies.

Modern technology was also introduced in heavy industry. The chemical, textile, metal and engineering industries saw rapid developments which lead to greater efficiency and productivity. Under Mao, steel production had been reduced to a virtual 'cottage industry', with scrap metal being melted down in virtually every village and town throughout the country.

During the Cultural Revolution Mao had clamped down hard on scientists and researchers. They had been described as 'capitalist roaders'—people who supported capitalism rather than remaining true to socialism. Mao imprisoned some of them, but most were sent to work as peasant labourers in the remote rural areas of China. Under the Four Modernisations, these scientists were restored to their old positions. Schools and universities were encouraged to help more people to graduate from the education system with modern qualifications. China also began research into and development of computers, semi-conductors, lasers and other products which had been ignored during the long years of Mao's regime.

Agriculture

Industry

THE FOUR MODERNISATIONS

SCIENCE & TECHNOLOGY

DEFENCE

Finally, China sought to develop its armed forces into a modern, well-equipped unit. There was little evidence to suggest that China wanted to take a more aggressive role in the world, but clearly Deng and the new leadership did not want to be left behind in the Arms Race at a time when the Cold War was still being acted out.

RECENT CHANGES IN THE CHINESE ECONOMY

The idea that any form of private enterprise could exist in China would have been unthinkable until recently. However, one of the effects of the Four Modernisations has been to encourage limited private enterprise and the result has been a boom in the Chinese economy.

This new thinking can be seen clearly in agriculture. At the time of the Cultural Revolution, all farming was organised in communes. Agricultural workers were paid a fixed wage regardless of how much they produced. This meant that there was little incentive to work hard, and therefore output was low. People took little pride in their work, and the quality of the crops produced was often very poor.

Since the late 1970s the communes have been abolished. The government still owns much of the land, but it rents out plots to individuals or families who want to work as farmers. Farmers must fulfil production agreements with the government, but any-

thing that is left over they can sell in markets for whatever price they can get. Some farmers have been quite successful and have seen a steady improvement in their living standards. They are allowed to invest in new machinery such as tractors and can build their own houses on their plots. The overall result has been to encourage people to work harder and to produce more. This means that some farmers have a much better lifestyle than before and the quality and quantity of agricultural products has improved.

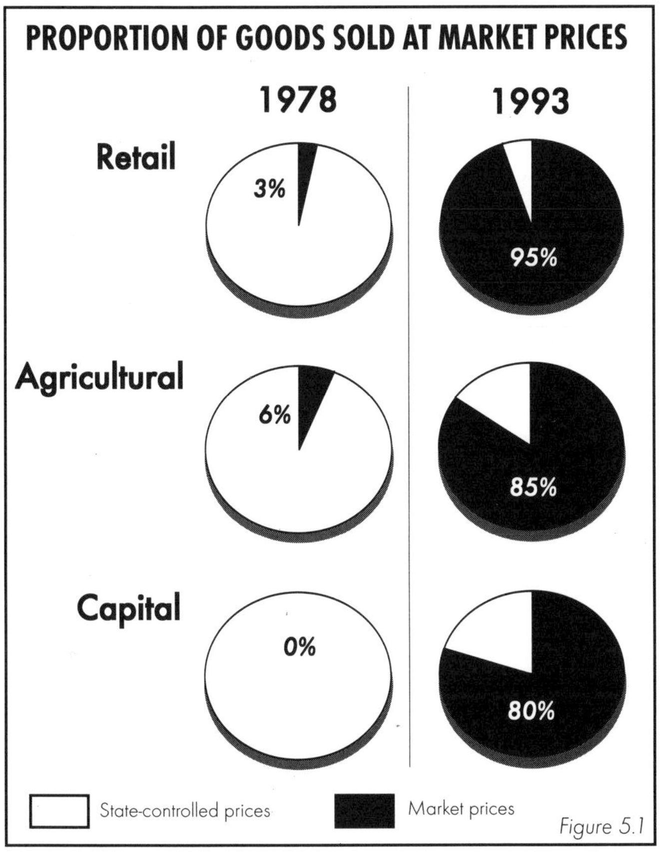

One consequence of this is that the more successful farmers tend to expand at the expense of the less successful. Fewer people are required to work on the land as farms become bigger and machines replace humans. In southern Hunan province alone, one million peasants have abandoned farming to become factory workers, migrating to the cities.

Deng Xiao   ping, when questioned about the way China has moved away from true socialist principles, answered, "It does not matter whether a cat is black or white, as long as it catches mice". In other words, in modern China the end result justifies the means. The switch away from Communist principles seems reasonable when the Chinese economy has made such giant strides.

THE EFFECT OF THE GREAT LEAP OUTWARDS

China has now become an important country in the international economy. Businesses from other countries often use China as a manufacturing centre. They go there for two main reasons. Firstly, wages are low which means that production costs can be kept down. An item of clothing, or a stereo system can be manufactured by workers who are paid a very low hourly rate compared to what would be demanded in Europe, North America or Japan. Secondly, the Chinese government offers large incentives to companies who are willing to set up factories in China. The administration in Beijing is conscious of the fact that recent changes in farming methods have left many former peasants without jobs. They have flocked to towns and cities in search of work, and many have ended up working in factories set up by foreign businesses.

China is no longer closed to foreigners. It is becoming more popular as a destination for tourists, who are fascinated by China's long and interesting history and unique culture. Tourists are welcomed by the government because they bring valuable hard currency into the country and provide a further boost to employment in many areas.

PROPORTION OF GOODS SOLD AT MARKET PRICES

1978   1993

Retail   3%   95%

Agricultural   6%   85%

Capital   0%   80%

☐ State-controlled prices   ■ Market prices

Figure 5.1

FACTFILE : China & Japan

CHINA AND JAPAN — RIVAL POWERS IN THE FAR EAST

Japanese industry has been recognised as being amongst the most efficient in the world. Over the last thirty years, Japanese products have become very common in homes in Britain. Japan has developed a reputation for producing top quality electrical goods, and also for good value cars.

China hopes to rival Japan's position as the major economic power in the Far East, but it still has a long way to go.

The figures below show the differences between the two countries.

- The population of China is ten times the population of Japan.

- China's population is growing by more than 1% per year; Japan's population is growing by less than 0.5% per year.

- People in Japan can expect to live ten years longer than the Chinese.

- In China the Infant Mortality rate is 31 per 1,000 live births, while in Japan it is 5 per 1,000 live births.

- Nearly one-quarter of Chinese adults cannot read or write. In Japan everyone is expected to learn to read and write during compulsory schooling.

- In Japan there is a telephone for every two people. In China there are 77 people to each telephone.

- Japan consumes six times as much energy as China.

- Japan has a well-organised political opposition, and also has terrorist groups who take direct action when they disagree with government policy. Political opposition in China is strictly controlled.

Activities

1 What were the features of 'The Four Modernisations' policy?

2 Why did Deng think that the 'Great Leap Outwards' was necessary to help China to make progress?

3 What are the special features of a 'Socialist Market Economy'?

4 What changes have taken place in Chinese agriculture?

5 Why are tourists particularly welcomed in China?

THE OPEN DOOR POLICY

China's leaders have been desperate to create economic growth in their country. This would have been very difficult if they had continued to maintain China's isolation from the outside world. By opening its doors China has been able to attract investment and new technology from abroad. The so-called 'Open Door' policy has taken a variety of forms which are outlined below.

1 *Special Economic Zones:* Areas have been set aside on China's South Eastern Coast, near to Hong Kong, Macau and Taiwan, where large incentives are offered to foreign businesses who are willing to move in. In special cases planning restrictions may also be removed.

2 *Super Trade Zones:* China used to be noted for the incredible bureaucracy involved in trying to establish trade links. In these zones Chinese businesses can deal directly with foreign businesses without having to go through any government department.

3 *Joint Venture Schemes:* These involve direct co-operation between foreign and Chinese companies. German car manufacturers, Volkswagen, have a Joint Venture Scheme with the Shanghai Tractor and Automotive Corporation, and Cadbury have a deal

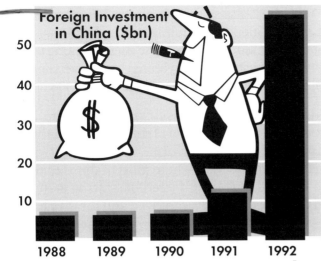

Figure 5.2

with the Beijing General Corporation for Agriculture, Industry and Commerce to produce chocolate in China.

4 *Ministry for Economic Relations and Trade:* The Chinese government has set up a whole Department specifically to encourage and develop trade links with other countries.

5 *New Laws and Financial Organisations:* To make investment by foreign companies easier, the Chinese government has passed various new laws. They have also set up a new Industrial and Commercial Bank, a Central Bank and an Agricultural Bank of China to encourage investment.

ECONOMIC SUCCESS IN THE NEW CHINA

There have been many notable economic advances in Deng's China. The important economic indicators such as industrial output, investment, share of world trade and exports have all shown significant annual rises.

In the countryside there has been an explosion of new industries. These have provided new jobs—an important point when so many peasants have lost their jobs in farming.

Farming itself has also shown rapid change. Although production of grain crops has fallen, there is now a wider variety of crops produced in China. The cultivation of cash crops has expanded, allowing farmers to improve their living standards. The fact that farmers can keep their own profits has allowed them to reinvest and buy consumer products previously unknown in the countryside.

China has become a consumer society. Advertisements for foreign products such as Coca Cola can be seen all over the country, and peasants and town dwellers alike are desperate to own the latest consumer goods.

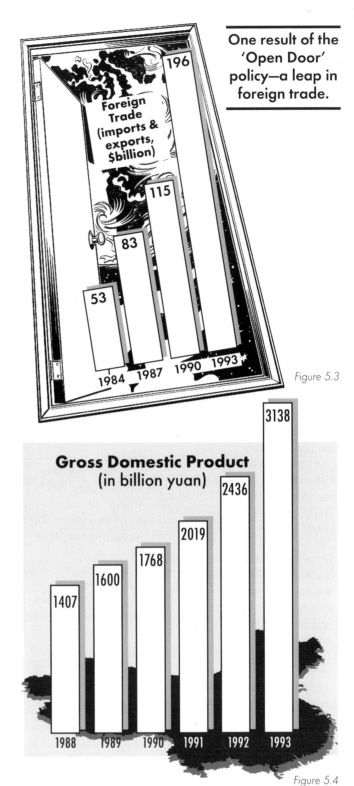

One result of the 'Open Door' policy—a leap in foreign trade.

Figure 5.3

Figure 5.4

111

China's Special Economic Zones

In 1980 the Chinese government established the first of the Special Economic Zones. The areas of Shenzen, Shantou, Xiamen and Zhuhai, along the southern coast near Hong Kong, were given special status. Hainan Island was added in 1988.

Chinese and foreign businesses can set up in these areas without many of the restrictions that apply elsewhere in China. The impact on Guangdong province, where most of these zones are situated, has been incredible. Living standards have been greatly improved and the area has been called a 'Mini Japan'.

Gibson has designs on China

POWER STATION design engineers Gibson Group of Glasgow are on the point of signing a £65 million contract to supply a 120-megawatt power station for Liaoning province in China.

Preliminary agreement has been reached and final negotiations will start in the next few weeks in the hope that a contract can be signed before Christmas, according to chairman and managing director Tom Gibson.

The group's contracting company, Gibson Wells Engineering, has been working on the project for three years. Gibson Wells has an impressive track record in the provision of power stations and automatic city traffic light systems for China — Chinese companies do not have the necessary technology to construct them.

Mr Gibson and group Commercial Manager Michael Ranson have recently returned from China after successful discussions in Beijing and visits to cities stretching from Manchuria in the north-east to the Vietnamese border in the south-west.

Mr Gibson said that the group had discussed a number of possible power station projects ranging from 100-megawatt to 700-megawatt stations, which are being planned for the near future and would involve business worth approximately £1,000 million.

He also disclosed that the group expected an agreement to be reached soon with a major US company which is looking to invest in power projects in China. Gibson Group is actively looking for Joint Venture Schemes to help finance contracts on such a large scale.

Adapted from *The Glasgow Herald* 7.10.93

CHINESE FORGE NEW LINKS WITH STRATHCLYDE

There were head-on talks in Glasgow yesterday on trade opportunities between Scotland and China when 70 representatives of Scots companies were able to discuss business directly with senior officials and business leaders from Guangdong Province.

Business group leader Wei You Lin, of the Guangdong sub-council for promoting international trade, told the Scots he was hopeful that the day's discussions with Scots businessmen would lead to co-operation in a number of production fields and would enhance the relationships already established between the two regions.

John Downie, assistant director of Strathclyde Business Development, said that Guangdong represented a massive opportunity for business. Its gross domestic product was rising by 22%, which was 10% higher than the average for China.

On a recent visit he had formed three lasting impressions. First, that the Chinese market was open for a wide range of manufacturing and service industries. Second, that the economic changes would continue despite some local ups and downs. And third, he had been very impressed by the enormous range of manufacturing abilities and the continuing search for quality in China.

Among the sectors under discussion were banking and finance, electronics and computer components, agriculture and various foodstuffs, food processing equipment, chemicals, hotel construction, supermarkets and department stores, textiles, tourism, sheet metal and building materials —all of which could be the subject of future Scottish-Chinese cooperation.

Adapted from *The Glasgow Herald*, 14.10.93

Activities

Read the article Gibson has designs on China .

1   What benefits will this project bring to
    a) Scotland?   b) China?

2   What is a 'Joint Venture Scheme' (see page 110)?

3   *"We are better prepared for this contract than any Chinese company."* (Tom Gibson)

    What evidence is there to suggest that Tom Gibson's statement is correct?

4   *"Our company is actively looking for more contracts in China."* Identify two pieces of evidence to back up this statement.

ECONOMIC PROBLEMS

Critics of Deng Xiaoping's policies would say that there have been more problems than successes. They would argue that many of the great social advances achieved since the revolution of 1949 have been wasted. The great principle of equality has been ignored as competition has been introduced to China.

Deng's policies have led to an increase in consumer demand which has caused prices to rise. Economists use the term 'overheated' to describe China's economy. This means that there is too much demand and too much growth. China cannot produce everything that the public are demanding, so imports have increased. In particular, consumer durables such as television sets, refrigerators, and hi-fi systems are imported on a vast scale.

The chaotic economic situation has allowed corruption and the black market economy to grow. Some people have become very rich under the new conditions, while others have been exploited in the process.

Deng's policies on farming may have increased the range and quality of the products, but they have also caused a number of problems. There has been a drop in the production of staple foods such as rice and in the long term this could lead to hunger. The land has been broken up into small plots, and in other countries this has been shown to be a bad system. Only the more successful farmers can afford the machinery needed for modern farming. In the old days these machines used to be shared by the peasant farmers on communes. The Chinese environment has been affected by the changes as less and less attention is paid to the problems of pollution and environmental decline. Major structural developments which were started in the 1960s and 1970s have now been halted—including projects such as new dams. The government is no longer prepared to spend money on such projects, and the new breed of farmers would not be able to afford them.

It remains to be seen whether the great economic changes introduced by Deng Xiaoping can actually address the fundamental problems of the Chinese economy. These remain:

1 *Feeding the population:* With over one quarter of the world's people and the possibility of a rising birth rate, producing and buying enough food is a major problem.

2 *Efficiency of production:* In such a huge country, with great cultural differences between regions, it has always been difficult to run the economy efficiently.

3 *Poor infrastructure:* Infrastructure means the road and railway network, telephones and telecommunications, water, electricity and gas supplies. China is a long way from having a modern system for any of these.

4 *Unskilled work force:* The Chinese work force is not skilled in the methods required for a modern economy.

5 *Trade deficit:* The links with other countries have simply made Chinese people more keen to buy goods from abroad.

6 *Poor quality production:* Although Chinese products have improved, they are still poor quality when compared to European, American or Japanese standards.

Activities

1 What is meant by the idea of an 'overheated economy'?

2 What are the main economic problems faced by China in the mid-1990s?

3 The graphs on page 111 show how much progress the Chinese economy has made in recent years.

What are the main trends shown in the graphs?

Study the sources below and answer the question which follows.

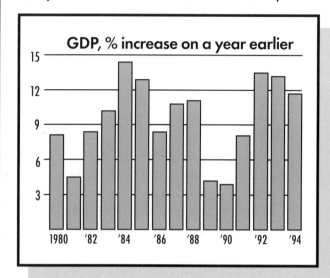

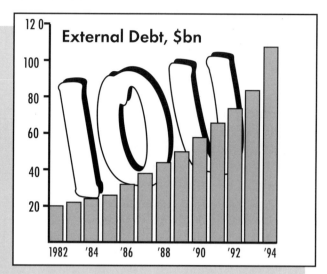

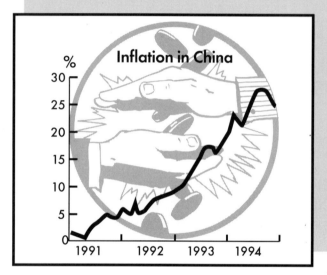

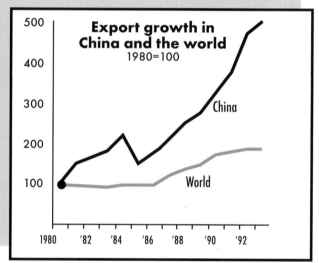

Source *The Economist*, A Survey of China, 18 March 1995

Inflation = The rate at which prices are rising

GDP = The total value of goods and services produced in the country in a year

External Debt = The amount of money which China owes to other countries

Exports = The value of goods sold by China to other countries in a year.

> *"China's economy has been a complete success in recent years.*
> *There have been no signs of any problems at all."*
>
> *View of a Chinese Economist*

Why could the Chinese Economist be accused of exaggeration? Give evidence from the sources to back up your answer.

THE CHINESE COUNTRYSIDE

What you will learn

1   How life in the countryside has been affected by recent changes in China.

2   The extent of the contrasts in living standards between urban and rural areas.

THE RESPONSIBILITY SYSTEM

The introduction of the Responsibility System was the most important part of Deng Xiaoping's economic changes. Under Mao Zedong, peasants had worked in Communes where they were paid a fixed wage regardless of how much was produced. This meant that there was no incentive to produce large quantities of good quality products.

In farming, the Responsibility System has introduced major changes.

- Plots of land are rented for private production.

- Decisions about what to produce and how much to produce are now made by individual peasants, rather than by the government.

- Peasants often get contracts to grow things for the government. Anything they grow above that amount can be sold on the open market.

- Peasants keep the profit from their land and can spend it in any way they want. Some will reinvest it in machinery and equipment, while others will buy the consumer goods which are now available.

The effect of these changes has been to raise living standards amongst the more successful farmers. However, there have been many people forced off the land as the more successful ones expand their businesses.

The choice and quality of food available to the ordinary Chinese people has increased.

In industry the main changes brought in by the Responsibility System have affected management. Under the new system, the management in a factory or business can:

- decide exactly what should be produced;

- decide the best production methods to make the factory more efficient;

- employ whoever they want—people are chosen for their technical ability rather than for their political correctness;

- have a say in deciding the prices which will be charged for their products.

The whole ideology of Chinese industry has changed. Under Mao, people worked to make China richer and more successful. Now the same people are not ashamed to say that they are working to make themselves richer and more successful.

Major Crop Production (1990)

Figures in thousand tonnes

Rice	188,403
Sweet Potatoes/Yams	112,220
Wheat	96,004
Maize	87,345
Sugar Cane	57,620
Potatoes	33,050
Sugar Beet	14,525
Soya Beans	11,508
Ground Nuts	6,368
Barley	3,100

Table 5.1

Agricultural Output (Cereals)

International Comparison, 1988

Figures in thousand tonnes

China	352,306
USA	206,467
Japan	20,983

Table 5.2

Agricultural Output (Meat)

International Comparison, 1988

Figures in thousand tonnes

China	24,996
USA	27,935
Japan	3,396

Table 5.3

NB China's population is approximately four times that of the USA.

Adapted from *Country Factfiles, China*, Simon and Schuster, 1994

There have been many positive developments as a result of the Responsibility System, but it has also brought a few problems to China. The pace of change has been very fast, and the differences between rich and poor have got wider. The environment has suffered as businesses seek bigger profits without consideration of the pollution and environmental problems which they are creating.

THE FREE MARKET ECONOMY

The idea of a 'Free Market' is unheard of under true Communism. It is an indication of the changes which have taken place in China recently that 'Free Markets' are now commonplace. Peasants can buy and sell their farm produce at free markets where the price is decided by the forces of supply and demand rather than by order of the government.

Chinese peasants used to sell all their produce to the government at a fixed price. Now if something is scarce then the peasant can get a higher price for it. Likewise if there is a surplus of something else, then the price of that product will fall.

Deng's aim in introducing a Free Market system was to encourage the peasants to produce larger quantities and a wider variety of products. This should make sure that China has an ample food supply, and that peasants have a chance to improve their lifestyles by selling products such as tobacco, cotton and other non-food crops.

THE CHINESE COUNTRYSIDE AND SIDELINE PRODUCTION

It was the Third Plenum of the Communist Party in 1978 that sparked off the great changes in China. For a few years afterwards the most notable changes took place in the countryside. More recently, the focus of change has switched to China's towns and cities.

The early success was linked to the introduction of the Responsibility System, which allowed farmers to have much more say in both what they produced and the methods they would use. Average incomes for farmers quickly rose, and the hated communes and government bureaucracy disappeared.

Farmers were still required to produce a certain quantity of grain crops for the government. However, they were paid a better price for the crops and they were also allowed to grow other crops for themselves and to keep the profits. The rural work force was happier and more motivated than it had been for many years.

Agricultural production reached a peak in 1984. Due to over-production, the government's price was cut slightly, and since 1984 output has remained steady. Many farmers switched to the production of 'sideline crops', such as eggs and vegetables.

Sideline production is a growing sector of the Chinese economy. It was only made possible by Deng Xiaoping's policies which encouraged farmers to produce their own crops on private plots.

The production of sideline crops multiplied in the 1980s. However, it should be noted that the incomes of the peasant farmers involved did not rise in line with this, mainly because the costs of production also increased rapidly.

Sideline Outputs in Rural China, 1978–1989

Product	1979	1984	1989
Pigs (Millions)	2	19	49
Fowls (Millions)	40	305	581
Eggs (Thousand Tonnes)	45	445	1446
Vegetables (Sown Area, Million hectare)	3.7	4.3	6.3

Source: *China: The Next Decades* (Ed. Dwyer, 1994)   *Table 5.4*

URBAN–RURAL CONTRASTS

Much of the economic success of recent years has been concentrated in the towns and cities. At the same time the Responsibility System has led to many smaller farmers losing their land and they have become poorer. Within the rural areas there is now a noticeable divide between the comparatively few successful farmers and the remainder. Overall, the countryside remains poorer than the urban areas.

The growing wealth of the towns has attracted many migrants. They cannot always find work or hous-

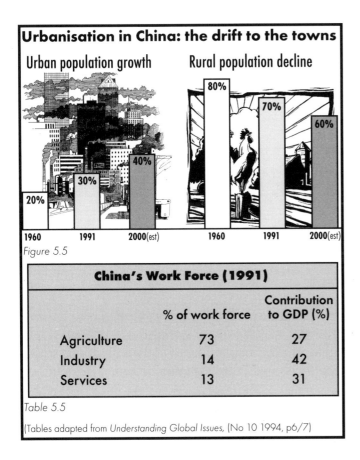

Urbanisation in China: the drift to the towns

Urban population growth — 20% (1960), 30% (1991), 40% (2000 est)

Rural population decline — 80% (1960), 70% (1991), 60% (2000 est)

Figure 5.5

China's Work Force (1991)	% of work force	Contribution to GDP (%)
Agriculture	73	27
Industry	14	42
Services	13	31

Table 5.5

(Tables adapted from *Understanding Global Issues*, (No 10 1994, p6/7)

Homes with selected consumer goods (per 1000 households)

- Urban households
- Rural households

Radios — 103 / 61

Televisions — 87 / 7

Sewing Machines — 77 / 43

Watches — 283 / 109

Bicycles — 163 / 74

Figure 5.6

ing and therefore live in poverty on the edges of the major urban areas. Consequently, although the urban areas are generally wealthier, they too display a real divide between the 'haves' and the 'have nots'.

The recent economic policies, with the introduction of free-market principles, have clearly created casualties as well as successes. These are acceptable as part of Deng's policy of 'Socialism with Chinese Characteristics', but would not be acceptable under the true principles of Communism as stated by the likes of Mao.

The government's economic policies have also created great regional contrasts in China. The regions on the south-eastern coast, especially Guangdong, have developed much more quickly than the rest of the country, with opportunities and living standards far in excess of those found in areas like central Asia, close to the Mongolian frontier.

Activities

1 What major changes have been made to farming under the Responsibility System?

2 What changes has the Responsibility System brought to factories and businesses?

3 **"The whole ideology of China has changed."**

What evidence is there to support this statement?

4 **"China is one of the world's most important agricultural nations."**

a) What evidence is there to support this statement?

b) Why are the figures for agricultural production on page 115 misleading?

5 How important was sideline production in China in 1989, compared to earlier years?

6 **"The development of China has not been even. Rural areas remain backward compared to urban areas."**

What evidence is there to back up this statement?

7 **"It does not matter if a cat is black or white, so long as it catches mice".**

This is one of Deng's most famous sayings. Explain what it means with reference to the Chinese economy.

The Chinese political system is very different from that of the United Kingdom or any other Western country. In China there is only one political party—the Communist Party. There is no opposition party as we have in this country. Furthermore, there are no general elections like those which occur all over Europe. However, it would be wrong to say that Chinese people cannot participate in the running of their country. They simply participate in a different way from the one that we would consider to be normal.

THE CHINESE COMMUNIST PARTY

The Communist Party controls every aspect of national life—from major policy decisions at national level about international trade and defence issues to minor decisions at local level in factories and on farms. However, in the last few years the Communist Party has been lessening its grip on these local decision making groups and allowing them more freedom to make their own choices and policies.

Unlike Britain where anyone can pay their subscription and join a political party, in China it is not possible simply to join the Communist Party. Membership is considered to be a great honour and people have to work very hard and prove themselves to be worthy before being allowed to join. It is thought that there are about 52 million members of the Chinese Communist Party—about 4.3% of the population. Very few young people are allowed to join the Party. Instead they become members of the Young Pioneers or the Young Communist Youth League, hoping to become full Communist Party members at a later date.

Membership of the Communist Party used to allow people all sorts of special privileges. It still does, but more and more people who are not Communist Party members can also enjoy a better living stand-

ard these days. This is because of the economic changes which have allowed more private enterprise and the availability of consumer goods which people simply could not buy before.

The top decision making body in the Chinese Communist Party is the Central Committee. All of the Politburo are members of the Central Committee. This is rather like the British Cabinet in that it has members representing the different government departments such as Defence, Agriculture, Industry and so on. The leader of the Party is the Chairperson of this group. Mao Zedong—often known as Chairman Mao—held this position from the revolution until his death in 1976. After Mao's death another older politician called Deng Xioaping emerged as the most important political leader, although he is only Vice Chairperson of the Party.

Below national level the Chinese Communist Party is also organised on Regional and Local levels. Party officials carry out the policies decided at national level and encourage the ordinary people to support the government in Beijing.

Organisation of the Chinese Communist Party
General Secretary
Standing Committee (approx. 7 members)
Politburo (approx. 14 members)
CCP Central Committee (approx. 340 members)
National Party Congress
Provincial Party Committees
District Organisation
City and Town Party Organisation
Party Sections in Workplaces
Party Members

THE STRUCTURE OF CHINESE GOVERNMENT

The National People's Congress (NPC) is the main parliament for China and it meets for two or three weeks every year. Virtually all its members are from the Communist Party. Delegates are elected from local congresses every five years.

The NPC discusses and approves major national policies and selects the main officials and groups to run the country. They make up the State Council, and are mainly prominent members of the Communist Party or retired officials from the Communist Party structure. In reality the Standing Committee and the Politburo of the Communist Party are the most powerful bodies in the country.

THE NEIGHBOURHOOD UNIT SYSTEM

Ordinary Chinese people are organised into units. These units exist in offices and factories where they are called Work Units. They also exist in villages and in streets where they are known as Neighbourhood Units. The Units discuss local issues and problems, and every member has the right to vote after the discussion. When a Unit has reached a decision, then all the members must abide by it. The Chinese Communist Party has always been very influential in these Units, with Party members usually occupying the most important posts such as Chairperson and Secretary. However, as in many other walks of life, the power of the Communist Party is not quite as strong as it used to be.

Neighbourhood Units can make decisions which we in Britain would see as being a total invasion of privacy. For example, the Unit can plan Birth Control policies, deciding when it is a woman's turn to become pregnant, so that the government's policy of small families is not challenged.

Units can also demand that people report the presence of any strangers in the area, or require people to spend their holidays or days off tidying up the local environment.

The Neighbourhood Unit policy has several advantages and disadvantages. These are outlined in the box above.

The Neighbourhood Unit : Friend or Foe?

✔ People have a strong sense of community—they feel that they belong and they take a pride in their area.

✔ People become less selfish and take more interest in the problems and happiness of the people who live around them.

✔ Crime is reduced, as people will be reported to the authorities if they break the law. In Western societies people often just ignore minor law breaking.

✔ Neighbourhood Units make sure that people who are poor or old are looked after by their fellow citizens.

✘ Basic individual freedoms are challenged.

✘ People tend to live very similar lives because they are afraid to stand out from the crowd.

✘ People are encouraged to report each other to the authorities for minor things.

✘ Young people are repressed. They are not allowed to make decisions for themselves or to grow up with their own opinions.

RECENT CHANGES IN CHINESE POLITICS

The Chinese Communist Party is now in a confused state. Approximately 75% of China's output now comes from private firms, yet the Party insists that the country is still run on Communist principles! Even while money-madness is sweeping China, the Party still produces slogans which promote socialist values.

Deng Xiaoping coined the phrase 'socialism with Chinese characteristics' to describe the current philosophy of the Party. This implies that the Chinese system is unique and that Deng has developed a new set of political and economic principles which are different from the original Communist ideals.

The power of the Communist Party has dwindled, especially in the countryside. The switch from the Commune system to the Responsibility System was described in Section 3 (see page 115). The Chinese Communist Party no longer controls the lives of China's 700 million farm workers in 4 million rural villages.

To boost employment in small towns and villages, the government set up Township and Village Enterprises (TVE). These have become very successful and profitable. They have also drifted out of the control of the government and the Communist Party, with decisions now being taken by businessmen and 'clans', an ancient Chinese family grouping.

The Work and Neighbourhood Units of the Communist Party have lost a great deal of their influence over people. In October 1994 the Central Committee announced a 'Resolution on the Strengthening of the Construction of the Party's Grassroots Organisations'. This is a giant effort to revive the 100,000 Party cells, many of which have been overrun by what the Communists describe as the "evil forces of capitalism, triads and Christianity".

There has also been a recent drive to remind the country of the controlling power of the Communist Party. In September 1994, the Central Committee issued a document with the impressive title *Several Opinions of the Communist Party of China's Central Committee Concerning the Further Strengthening and Improvement of Moral Education in Schools*. This was an order to schools to remind pupils about the power of the Communist Party. Banners with slogans such as 'Long Live the Chinese Communist Party' have been displayed.

Obviously the leaders of the Communist Party are worried that their power has been reduced at grassroots level. So far they have been successful in preventing any opposition political movements from arising, but at times this has needed force as was seen at Tiananmen Square in 1989. (see page122)

THE FUTURE?

Deng Xiaoping is unlikely to live beyond the end of the 20th century. His likely successor is Jiang Zemin who would continue with the same sort of policies that Deng has introduced. These allow the Chinese people to participate more in economic decisions, but still do not give them any real political decision making power.

However, there are other groups waiting on the sidelines. There are hard-line Communists who would return to the policies of Mao Zedong, with the Communist Party again dominating every aspect of individual's lives. The ability of the people to participate would be greatly reduced.

There are also pro-democracy movements, although they have to remain 'underground' because of the reaction of the government. It is possible that they could once again emerge and present a challenge to the Communist leadership. This could lead to real improvements in the rights of the Chinese people to participate in decision making in what is the world's most populous country.

Activities

1   List some ways in which the Chinese National People's Congress is different from Parliament in Britain.

2   What are the most powerful political bodies in China?

3   How would a young person go about becoming a member of the Chinese Communist Party?

4   Why do so many people want to become members of the Party?

5   ***"The Neighbourhood Unit system has various advantages and disadvantages."***

    Summarise the main advantages and disadvantages of the system, and give your own opinion of whether you think it is a good system or not. Explain your answer.

6   Why will Chinese Communist Party leaders be worried that they might lose their grip on power?

CHAPTER 5

CHINA – SECTION 5

PROTEST AND RIGHTS IN CHINA

What you will learn

RIGHTS IN CHINA IN THE EIGHTIES

In earlier sections you learned about some of the changes which have taken place in China over the last fifteen years or so. These have happened under the leadership of Deng Xiaoping. However, all of these changes have been to do with the economic and social life of China. There have been no real changes to the political system, and the Chinese people are still denied many basic human rights.

It would seem natural that, when so many changes have taken place to the economy and in everyday life, similar changes should also have happened in politics. However, the Chinese Communist Party has been determined to hold on to power and has stood in the way of political change.

In 1980 the Chinese Constitution was changed, removing four important rights. Before then Chinese people had been entitled to speak out freely, to air views freely, to hold debates and to express their opinions by writing wall posters.

At the trial of Wei Jingsheng (see profile page 123), one of the leaders of the Democracy Movement at the time, an official statement was read out, saying that China should return to four basic principles:

- ☙ insisting on the socialist road;
- ☙ dictatorship of the proletariat (working people);
- ☙ leadership by the Communist Party;
- ☙ supremacy of Marxism-Leninism-Mao Zedong thought.

It was stated clearly that the Chinese people had the freedom to support these principles, but not the freedom to oppose them.

The reasons why the Democracy Movement rose again in 1989 were simple. The student leaders of the movement could see the conflict which existed between the economic changes and the failure of the Communist Party to reform the State. The increasingly capitalist economy was at odds with the communist system. The 'new rich' entrepreneurs were battling against the bureaucracy. The new educated and cultured elite could not live with the state-controlled media and educational system. All these factors combined to make people unhappy with the political system.

THE DEMOCRACY MOVEMENT OF THE LATE 1980s

The events of Tiananmen Square in June 1989 horrified the world. Hundreds, and possibly even thousands, of demonstrators were killed by government soldiers as they protested against years of political repression.

The Democracy Movement was made up of various groups within China who had benefited from the economic and social changes along with those who were fed up with the corruption which plagued the Communist political system.

The leaders of the Democracy Movement were students, some of whom had been given the opportunity to study abroad. They had seen the rights given to people in Western democratic systems. The students were the intellectual leaders of the Democracy Movement, but they drew support from other groups. The people who had become rich under the economic reforms had a taste for more political power. Ordinary workers who saw the extent of corruption amongst Communist officials formed the Workers Autonomous Union. Teachers and lecturers tended to support the Democracy Movement, as did journalists on some of China's newspapers.

The response of the Chinese Communist Party to the Democracy Movement displayed its determination to hold on to political power. The government and the Party used the People's Liberation Army to clamp down on all protests.

Martial Law (Military Rule) was imposed, with the army taking over from the police in Beijing and other major cities. The army was used to clear public areas of any demonstrators or protesters. Certain organisations, including the Students Union and the Workers Autonomous Union, were made illegal. Any politicians who had shown the slightest sympathy for the Democracy Movement were sacked. Ringleaders of the Democracy Movement were arrested. Newspapers which supported the Democracy Movement were closed down, and a major propaganda campaign was launched to portray the Democracy Movement leaders as enemies of the people.

It must be remembered that these events were taking place at the same time as the Communist regimes of Eastern Europe were crumbling, and Mr Gorbachev was implementing a far-reaching set of reforms in the Soviet Union, the world's other major Communist power.

Demands of The Democracy Movement

- Resignation of Prime Minister Li Peng
- Investigation into corruption in government
- Establishment of a Free Media
- Establishment of Free Trade Unions

THE EVENTS OF TIANANMEN SQUARE

In late April 1989, students occupied the main square in Beijing around the Monument to the People's Heroes. The occupation of the square was prompted by the funeral for a reforming leader called Hu Yaobang, who was regarded as a hero by the students. Throughout May support for the students grew from all over China, and the world's attention turned to the demonstrations in Beijing.

The Communist leadership showed no sign of giving in to the demands of the students, so a group of the leaders of the protesters began a hunger strike. On 31 May the students unveiled a new statue in the square, based on the American Statue of Liberty.

On 4 June specially selected sections of the Chinese People's Liberation Army attacked the demonstrators and pushed them out of the square. Reports on how many were killed and injured vary, but it is now generally accepted that about 2,000 were killed and 10,000 injured. The students did not fight back and many were crushed under the advancing tanks and armoured cars.

Martial Law continued until the following January, by which time all the political enemies of Deng Xiaoping and Li Peng had been removed from their jobs in the universities, factories and newspapers. There was a huge purge of the Communist Party membership. Anyone with the slightest connection with the Democracy Movement was thrown out of the Party, and anyone who had expressed support for them was arrested. Jiang Zemin, who replaced the reformer Zhao Ziyang as Secretary of the Communist Party, was quoted as saying:

> "That the socialist system will replace capitalism is the true trend of history. We are fully confident in the communist future of the human race. Hostile foreign forces and opposition within China to the Communist Party are completely bankrupt. The test of quelling the counter-revolutionary turmoil has proved that the Party is correct and strong."

Chinese students demonstrate by 'occupying' a war memorial in Beijing in 1989.

PROFILE OF WEI JINGSHENG

OCCUPATION: Electrician at Beijing Zoo

BACKGROUND

In the late 1970s, the Chinese government relaxed its control over the media. Wei was involved in writing articles for magazines which criticised the government, and he helped to produce wall posters which expressed the views of ordinary people.

One of Wei's articles was called *The Fifth Modernisation*, in which he called for the government to follow up the Four Modernisations with the introduction of democracy.

ARREST AND TRIAL

Wei was arrested in October 1979 and charged with editing a magazine not approved by the government and also with passing secrets to foreigners. The trial took place in private and he was found guilty after just seven hours. He was sentenced to fifteen years in prison.

CONDITIONS

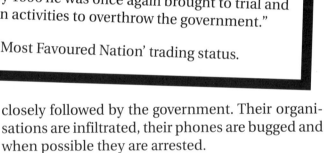

Wei was imprisoned with hardened criminals and his mental health broke down. In 1984 he was transferred to a mental hospital. He was released from prison in 1993 but rearrested on 1 April 1994. In January 1996 he was once again brought to trial and sentenced to another 14 years in prison for "engaging in activities to overthrow the government."

Despite Wei's imprisonment, the USA still gives China 'Most Favoured Nation' trading status.

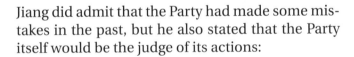

Jiang did admit that the Party had made some mistakes in the past, but he also stated that the Party itself would be the judge of its actions:

> "The Party has made mistakes over the past 40 years—we must relentlessly analyse and resolutely correct the mistakes in our work so as to solve problems within our Party."

In December 1989, the Communist Party announced the results of the inquiries into the aftermath of the Tiananmen Square demonstrations. 350,000 Chinese people had been 'disciplined'. Of those only 2,500 had actually been arrested, and about 2 dozen had been executed. 2,200 had been sent to Labour Camps, and another 300 had been fined. These 'official figures' are likely to be seriously underestimated.

HUMAN RIGHTS IN THE NINETIES

In the mid-1990s there are few active dissidents in China. However, those people who are active are closely followed by the government. Their organisations are infiltrated, their phones are bugged and when possible they are arrested.

The main dissident movement, led from prison by Wei Jingsheng, is the Labour Alliance, which campaigns for an end to special privilege, a limit to excessive powers, protection for human rights and a fair division of wealth.

The Labour Alliance claims to have widespread support in the country, with a frontline of open activists who are prepared to be arrested. If they are, then they have a second and third line of activists ready to come forward.

An American-based human rights group, Asia Watch, claims that political repression in China is increasing. Asia Watch recognised that a small number of political prisoners had been released in 1993, but felt that they were simply 'bargaining chips' in an attempt by the Chinese government to retain 'Most Favoured Nation' trading status with the United States of America.

The release of a few individuals has to be balanced against the fact that more than a million Chinese are detained every year without ever appearing before a court. Chinese police often use 'shelter and investigation' as a means of controlling the population. This policy allows people to be detained for up to three months, and it is used as a warning against certain activities.

The other main form of detention is 're-education through labour'. This allows people to be arrested and detained for up to three years without trial. Human rights monitoring groups claim that at any given time at least 100,000 people are being held under this system. Human rights reports also highlight the use of torture in Chinese jails, widespread capital punishment and the practice of publicly parading those on their way to execution.

THE CHINESE LAOGAI

The Chinese government uses the huge prison population as a labour force. The Laogai is the name given to the network of prisons, labour camps and 'hospitals' which exists in China. It is a vast network in which millions of prisoners are held and forced to work on behalf of the state. It totally ignores human rights, with torture, squalor and degradation the norm. China refuses to give accurate figures for its prison population, but conservative estimates put it at between 10 and 20 million. Up to half a million of these are political prisoners rather than criminals.

All the camps have two official identities. Firstly, they have a public face as an ordinary farm or factory. Secondly, they have their true name within the Laogai system. For example, Shanghai Number Seven Labour Reform Prison is also known as the Shanghai Laodong Steel Pipe Factory.

The basis of the Laogai rests on twin planks: hard labour and political 'thought reform'. The similarity to the Nazis' 'Freedom Through Work' slogan is not difficult to see. In China all prisoners are forced to work, the idea being that through forced labour they will remake themselves into new men who will embrace Communism and the socialist system.

Under Deng Xiaoping's guiding principle of 'Socialism with Chinese Characteristics', labour reform camps have been urged to become self-financing. Prisoners have always been required to work—now they are required to meet strict production quotas and targets. Failure to meet them results in savage beatings.

THE DEATH PENALTY IN CHINA

No fewer than 65 crimes carry the death penalty in China, including embezzlement, corruption and 'hooliganism'. Mass sentencing rallies still take place as a way of threatening the rest of the population and setting an example that will deter them from crime.

Condemned prisoners are paraded through the streets carrying banners which detail their crimes. Afterwards they are shot in the back of the head. It has been alleged that following execution their organs are removed for use in transplant operations.

Evaluating Exercise

STUDY THE SOURCES BELOW AND ANSWER THE QUESTION WHICH FOLLOWS

SOURCE A

Half a million political prisoners are rotting in China's penal colonies. Five years after the Tiananmen Square massacre, tourists visiting China are greeted by crudely-lettered slogans on rusty corrugated iron 'A More Open China Awaits You'. Many of China's political prisoners are forced to work in factories, producing goods for export to other countries to earn hard currency. Asia Watch's Robin Munro says, "There are references in internal Chinese government documents to individual prison factories exporting to over 30 countries around the world. China earns several hundred million dollars every year from prison labour."

Adapted from The Guardian, 24 July 1993

SOURCE B

China's prison system is one of the best in the world. Prisoners are taught about the best way to organise the economy in China, and they work in factories to make the prisons self-financing. The items produced in prison factories are only sold within China and are not used for foreign trade.

Official Chinese Government Source

From the information given in the two sources above, what different views exist about the purpose of the Chinese Prison Factory system?

Activities

1 What constitutional rights were taken from the Chinese people in 1980?

2 (a) Outline the demands of the Democracy Movement and describe the events of Tiananmen Square.

   (b) What further action did the government take to restore order?

3 Why is Wei Jingsheng China's most important political prisoner?

4 Describe life in a Chinese Laogai.

5 Why is China criticised for its use of the death penalty?

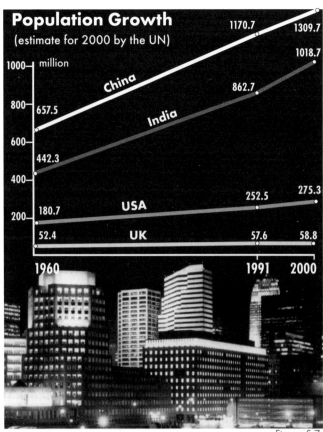

Figure 5.7

THE ONE CHILD POLICY

The *One Child Policy* of the Chinese government has often been used to show how it has interfered with basic human rights. With a population of over one billion and increasing by 25 every minute, one of the major problems of the government was to control the size of the population in order to relieve the severe strains on the economy. (see Figure 5.7)

Various social and economic measures were introduced to try and reduce the rise in population.

🚶 *Financial measures* – families with one child get all the state benefits, but a family with more than one child loses them.

🚶 *Abortion* – the government approves of, and indeed orders, abortions in many areas.

🚶 *Birth Control* – neighbourhood family planning teams hold education classes and clinics. Contraceptives are issued through the health system.

🚶 *Government Propaganda* – promoting the idea that small families are best

🚶 *Infanticide* – the practice of killing female children still goes on in some rural areas, where sons are prized and daughters are not wanted.

China has the strictest family planning policy in the world. Each couple is allowed one child and great pressure is brought to bear to abort a second pregnancy. The policy has had some success in reduc-

ing the birth rate, but the biggest drop in the rate has come about because of better living standards and the widespread availability of effective birth control methods.

In many rural areas the one-child policy has not worked. Peasants have simply ignored the rules, because they feel that they need other children to help them to work the land, and to look after them in their old age. They are prepared to pay the fines that result from having more than one child.

The policy has had social ill-effects as well. The single children are sometimes called the 'Little Emperors' because so many of them are spoiled and antisocial. In the more remote areas, female children are sometimes killed by their families at birth because male children are considered to have more 'prestige'. Consequently, there is an imbalance in the ratio between young men and young women in some parts of China.

The recent economic changes should help to reduce the birth rate. As China becomes more of a consumer society, parents will choose to have smaller families because of the financial factors. The availability of many western-style consumer goods means that people will not want to have such large families as they would prove to be a drain on their resources.

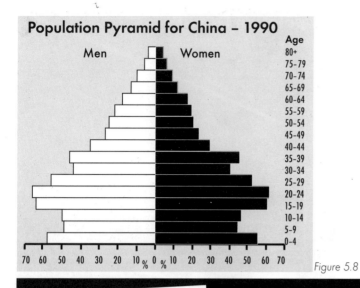

Population Pyramid for China – 1990

Men | Women

Age
80+
75-79
70-74
65-69
60-64
55-59
50-54
45-49
40-44
35-39
30-34
25-29
20-24
15-19
10-14
5-9
0-4

70 60 50 40 30 20 10 % 0 % 10 20 30 40 50 60 70

Figure 5.8

Activities

1   What measures has the Chinese government taken to control the size of the population?

2   How successful has the policy been and why has it been criticised?

3   **"China has solved her population problem."**

Using figures 5.7 and 5.8 state if you agree with the above opinion.
Give reasons for your answer.

Abortion in China

ABORTIONS have become routine in China. Up to five months into pregnancy they are performed by suction. From then until birth abortions are induced by doctors.

The major drawback of this approach is that babies are usually born alive. "It was upsetting to see a four or five-pound baby thrown into a trash can still alive," says Chi An, a former nurse in a Chinese hospital.

An alternative was injecting a powerful herb into the womb—poisoning the baby and inducing miscarriage. One doctor, says Chi An, induced birth and as the infant's head apeared injected lethal formaldehyde into its brian through the soft spot in its head.

The Chinese state employs strict sanctions to enforce the one child policy. 'Cheating' can bring severe punishment —pregnant women may find electricity and water supplies cut off from their house and in extreme cases houses have been pulled down.

Adapted from *The Herald*, 14 June 1995

Quality not Quantity

China has an estimated 4.2 million children who suffer from various forms of handicap. The whole country has just 100 schools to cater for handicapped children, and they can find places for only about 100,000 of them.

Professor Xiao Fei of Beijing University, an expert in the problems of the mentally handicapped, says, "If we can limit the number of these kids, then the country will shed some of its burden".

From 1 June 1995 the new Maternal and Infant Health Care Law came into force. This law bans marriages between people who have genetic diseases unless they agree to sterilisation or long-term contraception. Doctors must also advise pregnant women to have an abortion if they suspect a hereditary disease or abnormality in the unborn child.

Adapted from *Newsweek*, 28 November 1994

Chinese Children and the Dying Rooms

TODDLERS strapped to bamboo seats with built-in potties rock mindlessly back and forth for hours on end. Babies are left unattended in cots soaked through with their own urine. In 100 degree heat, with viruses rampant, infants are strapped five to a bed. One in five will die.

Almost all the infants in the orphanage are girls. Abandoned by their parents, they are the victims of China's one child policy and the preference of Chinese people for sons rather than daughters. Hundreds of thousands of infants are abandoned every year and many end up in orphanages like this.

They suffer from neglect and disease. Gangrene, malnutrition, vitamin deficiency … eventually the children become so weak that they die.

When it becomes obvious that they will not live they are strapped into chairs in the dying rooms and left.

Adapted from *The Herald*, 14 June 1995

China's Government Controls Births

Since 1993 the Chinese government has extended its one child policy.

Beijing decides on the overall number of children to be born. That is divided across 29 provinces down to villagers who are told how many babies they are allowed. Locally the Women's Federation Head and the local Party Secretary are responsible for ensuring that the quotas are met. For every baby over the quota they are docked between 5% and 10% of their salary. This means that if she has no permit for a child, even a childless woman will be forced to have an abortion.

Comparing the number of male and female children in China at present it seems as if some 15 million female babies have 'disappeared' in recent years. Some estimates say that up to 1.7 million female foetuses are being aborted each year.

Adapted from *The Herald*, 14 June 1995

Stories of what the One Child Policy meant in practice shocked readers of Western newspapers